MEMOIRS OF A
REBEL

BLACK MARKET SHOOTING

KON GEORGIOU

Memoirs of a Rebel
Copyright © 2021 by Kon Georgiou

Tellwell Talent
www.tellwell.ca

ISBN
978-0-2288-3581-3 (Paperback)
978-0-2288-3582-0 (eBook)

DEDICATION

I dedicate this, to Pass, Present and Future Outlaws.

TABLE OF CONTENTS

AUTHOR'S NOTE

I hope you all enjoy my book. I never had any intention of writing that but when I was told by the Governor of the Supermax I wasn't allowed to do it. Well, that was it for me. I was determined to do it no matter what. I am not a writer and I don't enjoy sharing my life with strangers, but once you tell me I can't do something, well this is what happens. Also, once I started putting my life on paper, I realised it will give the readers a better understanding of the Bike culture.

Over the years, many people ask me why? Why do you do the things you do? I always answer them with a rendition of one of my favourite fables, The Turtle and the Scorpion. I would like to share that with you.

On a dark and rainy day, a scorpion sits on a small mound in the middle of a river and as the rain falls the river starts to rise leaving less and less room on the mound for the scorpion. It is only a matter of time before the water covers the mound and the scorpion drowns. In a last-ditch attempt, the scorpion calls out to a turtle swimming by, "Turtle! Turtle! please help me, I am going to drown, let me jump on your back so I can get to the bank of the river". The turtle stops and calls back to the scorpion, "No! No! you are a scorpion and as soon as you jump on my back you will sting me," the scorpion replies. "But turtle, if I do that, we will both die" the turtle thought about this for a minute and replied "Ok scorpion, I will help you, but remember if you sting me, we will both drown." The scorpion was so happy as he jumped on the turtle's shell. Halfway across the river the scorpion whips his stinger and hits the turtle in the neck. The turtle turns his head looks at the scorpion and says "but why scorpion? Now we both die," the scorpion looks at the turtle and says, "I am sorry Turtle, I am sorry, but I am a scorpion and it's in my nature."

The moral of my fable is that I am a Rebel, and it's in my nature!

PROLOGUE

When you are surrounded by four white walls, especially when such situation is inevitable, you don't really have anything else to do except to stare at the walls. Sometimes you may try to shut off reality by closing your eyes, or even sleeping; but eventually even sleep will elude you. You will find yourself back again to that initial same situation, staring at the paint that has begun to chip off as years passed. On some occasions, you find the signatures left behind by other occupiers before you. The walls become your only plaything; you start to try to chip off the remaining paints glued to them or try to leave behind your own impression too – anything to pass time. And if this continues for too long you will begin to lose yourself, you will feel the sanity slipping away. That is when you will begin to theorize absurd meanings from the blank stare the walls return to you. You begin to see faces that are not there; ultimately you will cling onto the belief that you are not alone. The truth is that solitude can mess with your sanity, especially if you have a weak mind.

I have no tape or ruler – well, considering my present situation, it's not a surprise – but I am almost certain that the room is barely spacious enough to accommodate a heavily pregnant woman. Even though I am not an artist, if given a pencil and a paper I can draw it to its minutest details. When you are familiar with something enough, it becomes a part of you and steals a space in your subconscious – especially when those little details have been gathering receptively in your mind for years and even decades. When all the space you have is merely in a hollow cube of solid concrete with only one way in and without the luxury of a window, tends to have a certain perspective on some things; but the worst case is when you have no idea about how much time has passed, or if it is day or night. Of course, that is how they want it to be for you; the hollow cube has been deliberately designed for the sheer purpose of disorientation. And if one is condemned to that kind of fate for so long, in time the occupier of such a cube could forget their own name – and the loss of self-identity is the first step towards the inevitable looming insanity. The architects, the contractors, the designers, the builders – they don't just build the cells, they also poured their own hatred and inhumanity into the design. Depending on the gravity of your crimes – or for a better expression, *charges* – the cell you are assigned could as well be nothing but a concrete coffin; every moment you spend in it could be freaking excruciating and maddening by expectation. The bastards who have put you in this hollow cube, this coffin, are looking forward to seeing your transform from a human being into an animal – or worse, a carcass.

Anyone who has been to a prison will always tell you that it's another world there. It's not just walls and fences and cells and locks and gates. The air smells differently; the ways of life there are also peculiar – the prison society is the perfect definition of dog-eat-dog world. It's a wasteland of the mind, an apocalypse of the psyche; and to survive you have to claw and strive with determination. You cannot afford to compromise, or the system is going to win, in a tremendous way at that. You have got to fight yourself free from that vicious, vice-like and icy grip of death and loneliness.

My cell is not like a regular, average cell. I choose to see it as a special box designed only for me alone, even though I know that it's not really true. It is 4.25 metres by 2.5 metres concrete and steel room. A 60-centimetre steel pole with a round metal disc the size of a dinner plate jutting out of the concrete floor. I'm sure the builders must have applied extra cement in the flooring of the cell; probably to prevent the intention of digging a tunnel through the floor. The pole is my seat – it is the only seat I have, and there is no seat for any guest – well, it's a cell, isn't it? Who would pay me a complimentary visit here? The seat is a few inches away from the wall; and each time I seat on it, my knees barely miss touching the wall. The architect had taken the careful steps in making sure that no space was wasted or left for pleasure – as the case may be.

Besides the seat that came from the floor, there was also a bench that is attached to the wall. Like the seat, it's immovable, unless you plan to move the wall with it. The bench is about 1.5 metres long and 30 centimetres wide. If you step into the cell through the entrance (which, of course, is the only avenue to entering the cell) you will find my sandwich maker and kettle on the left-hand side; and on my right are my containers with my coffee, tea, skimmed milk powder and sweetener. We are only get issued sweetener because with real sugar you can make alcohol.

The space above my head bears a steel box with a Perspex front so that inmates can see the TV entombed in it. Only the powers-that-be have access to the channels. I can't even touch it; all I can do is watch whatever is displayed on the screen, and of course everything displayed is regulated. There is no luxury of CNN or Foxtel here. Most of the stuff being displayed on the screen could bore you to death since majority of them are meant to reform you. To me, it seems like a lame attempt at making the prisoner become a better person. Believe me, TV does little to reshape inmates.

At the right side of where I sit, just at the end of my bench, is a 2.1-metre-high metal shelving unit that contain six shelves for my clothes, food, stationery and toiletries; and behind me is my bed, a solid steel rectangular box; the steel seemed like something cut from a shipping container, and on it is a 10-centimetre-thick piece of foam covered in fire resistant material – the foam obviously serves as my mattress. Well, I guess I should consider myself fortunate. Things could have been worse for me; there are prisons where the inmates do not have the luxury of mattress – they have only the steel bed to lay themselves on.

At the end of my bed, towards the back of the room, is my shower. The shower is an open one; there is no curtain or any form of covering – nothing divides it from the room. Each time I use it, I have to wipe the entire cell of steam and over splash afterward. Prisoners are beggars; they don't choose. There's nothing like privacy. Whenever I'm using the shower and a guard passes by my cell, they will see me clearly in my birthday suit – but then again, who really cares about decency in prison? Nobody cares. Just make sure you don't drop the soap, that's one thing I don't have to worry about in solitary confinement.

Beside the shower is my toilet and sink, which are made of equally solid stainless steel. No prison will provide its inmates with ceramic toilet that could easily be broken, and its shard used for a weapon. My toilet has no seat, nothing detachable – everything is metal. I am too familiar with the coldness of the steel on my rear each time I make use of it. On the sink is a big roll of tissue. This, I have an abundance of. Sometimes the toilet paper is not only used for cleaning up but it can also be used to write messages on it. As soon as the message is read, the paper can be dropped in water where it would dissolve immediately and the message will be safely disposed of forever. The way these messages are passed on are by way of a line. We unweave threads from our blankets and make a long line, long enough to reach the cell we want the message to get too. We do this by adding a small thin weight on the end of the line that can slide under the door gap and we slide the weight towards the cell we want to reach and the occupant of that cell will try and fish it in with his line. This can sometimes take hours to achieve, but one thing we have is plenty of time. Now back to outlining my cell.

At this moment as I sit here writing this note, there is a steel door that can be unlocked in the day so that I can have access to what I consider a 'back yard'. This space is barely half the size of my room, and it is covered in a metal cage within a cage. This is how I gain access to sunlight whenever I'm lucky enough to open the cage, which is not all the time. Sometimes I am not allowed this access because the door is occasionally electrically locked. At my right-hand side is my front door which is also made of reinforced steel that not even The Incredible Hulk could break down. The other side of this door is another community on its own because it represents a cacophony of different sounds – screaming, laughing, throwing expletives, preaching, doors being kicked and some people making animal noises.

There is something eerily disturbing about this place I am in; the right descriptions elude me, but it seems like it has been engineered with a precision to torment, or the attempt thereof. I couldn't tell if it was the walls or the steel door. The person who created this place must have sat in a very comfortable office to think about how he could make this place as soulless as possible; how he could create it in a manner that its occupier would not enjoy the faintest sense of pleasure. The person, ingenious with his talent, had contemplated on every little detail and had left no stone unturned no matter how minute it was; and, of course, no turn *unstoned*. For the person, stripping the freedom off the inmate was apparently not enough; he wanted to take more, something he had no right to take – and he chose to take it by designing this prison. It wasn't our sanity; it's something deeper than that, darker – yet I can't point to what it is. You can have your sanity and everything else, but when you get out you will know a part of you has been left behind in this place. I am having that feeling.

My description might have planted in your mind the thought that I was in a mental asylum for the criminally insane. Well, you might not be too far from the truth. This is High Risk Management Unit (HRMU) Goulburn Supermax. My name is Konstantinos Georgiou and I am a born rebel.

It is February 2020 and I have spent 22 years out of my 31-year-sentence. My last 15 years have been at the Supermax in solitary confinement. Do not have pity on me. I don't want anyone's sympathy – in fact, I have no sympathy for myself. All I want is for you to read this so that you can have a better understanding of why people like me do what we do, and what makes us who we are.

If we all contemplate life, love, despair, happiness and loss as I have been able to do for the last few years of my life, then we can all accept that we don't choose the paths we have taken. The coordinate is written in our heads. Whether your gay, straight, white, black – it's not a choice. Whatever step we take, the choices we make the paths we tread – they have all been conditioned into our subconscious. Sometimes even when that choice is the wrong one, and we know it, we realize we can't stop ourselves from taking those steps. So, I will implore you to not be quick to judge your fellow man or woman; instead, look inward first. Perhaps by doing that you will get a semblance of what pushed that person to take that action.

Okay, before I get too philosophical for my own good, let me explain the circumstances that led me to this place – to this moment.

1

KINGS CROSS

I have always known that I am someone who constantly seeks adventure. I like to see myself as an interesting person; I abhor a boring place or situation because for my whole life I have always looked for that next thrill that would give me the adrenaline rush I so badly needed to feel alive – something that would keep my mind and body racing at a fast pace. It could be speeding through an intersection at 160km/hour or climbing a 10-storey building after three days of drinking just to surprise a friend. I would do anything to get that rush. Indeed, some of these adventures have damn near claimed my life or put me in some serious trouble with the authorities, but, well, that's the idea. What could get the adrenaline pumping besides danger? It's my way of letting myself know that I am still alive and not just living. I would rush into places where even angels fear to tread, and I am hardly scared of anything. I live my life under one philosophical rule. If it's not your time, even the apocalypse will not kill you. I'm not suicidal or anything; I don't have so much confidence about my safety that would make me erect myself before a speeding locomotive. That's not adventure – it's plain stupidity, or even insanity. I guess what I'm simply trying to say is that I am not afraid to take risks, for life itself is an embodiment of risks.

My story begins in Kings Cross in the mid 90's. I had been working there on and off since the 80's; but at a time, I left to carve a new life for myself. However, after a failed relationship I returned to Kings Cross. My major reason for leaving in the first place was to have a normal, ordinary life like most of the respectable folks out there. I know that wasn't my kind of life; I just wasn't programmed to live that way but I wanted to try my hands at being a responsible person for once by running a small business, getting engaged to a good girl and trying to settle down. However, as hard as I tried, I wasn't cut out for that kind of life. I finally threw in the towel after one year – it just wasn't working for me. I felt like I was losing myself; like an atheist who had been forced to go to church, you will always question everything the preacher says. I began to question the rationality behind living a normal life, for in my dictionary, 'normal' is the synonym of boring. And if I continued to live my life like that, I would die before my time. My death would be pathetic; it would be downright humiliating. After one year, I knew I had to get out before it became too late for me.

So, I subconsciously sabotaged the relationship I had with the girl; I also suspended my initial plan to set up a small business. I would be damned if I lived off that kind of business when I knew that there were other interesting things I could do and earn a lot more. Leaving my girl in the lurch, I hooked up with a couple of strippers and returned to Kings Cross. I went to Fatty, my underworld uncle who owned half the strip clubs on the main strip. I started by working for him; I would bring him new girls to work the clubs and he would pay me what the girls would earn. So, if one girl would make $300 a night, Fatty would pay me $300 as well just for looking after them and making sure they showed up for work. I had two strippers working the strip clubs on the strip two to three days a week.

Finding strippers isn't really hard, money talks. Girls who are willing are all around you; you only have to tell them how much money they can earn and the rest is history. You can pick up girl's night clubs or bars. A lot of them would jump at the opportunity to become strippers at reputable clubs. And when you've got their interest, you can make a deal that would be very profitable for you and the girls. Other guys in this line of work prefer amateurs or the rookies who are eager to make it; these ones are easy to herd around like sheep, and they will take whatever you offer them. They are not very expensive when you manage to catch them young. And with just a little training they are in business. But in my kind of business, I didn't need amateurs; I used to pick professionals and specific kinds of girls – you've got to have standards, especially when you are dealing with someone like Fatty. He wouldn't accept just any girl; that's why I had only two really good strippers for him. It was easy money; I didn't have to do anything much; I only had to make sure the girls were safe and always showed up whenever they were needed. If you know your way around the Cross, whatever you do there is easy money.

People who do not know their worth are the ones always working so hard to earn peanuts. They are the ones who wouldn't mind working twelve hours to earn what I can make in five minutes. And why is that? It's because they want to continue following the system – the right way, the legal way. They will sweat and release snots but have nothing to show for it at the end of the day. I couldn't believe that was the kind of lifestyle I was ready to engage myself in. I wanted to give up this opportunity to slave my life away for something that wasn't worth it after all. I must have been under a form of spell to even consider that thought.

Besides managing two strippers, I was also in charge of three runners for a guy called DK. Runners was the street name given to the people selling drugs. Let it be understood that these were only foot soldiers; their job was just to sell drugs. The sell and hand in a certain amount. It's pretty basic. Let's say, for instance, they are given drugs worth of $100 to sell and they are able to sell it for $130 or $150, depending on their trading power – or business sense, as you may call it. They get to hand in the $100 and keep whatever extra is made from it. In some cases, the profit they make in selling the drugs is different from the payment they also receive for their services. Like I said, it's easy money.

My job, in this regard, is to look after the night shift and make sure the runners are not robbed by junkies or crooks. In some very rare occasions, some runners might try to act smart by falling short on their payment or absconding with the money. This is often a very dumb thing to do. Many runners have lost their lives by thinking this way; or they lose either an arm or a leg in the very least. Besides that, whenever any of the runners was robbed, one of them would find me on the main strip or in Dancer's night club where I would usually stay, and I would handle the situation. I knew basically everyone in the neighbourhood, and I consider myself a good tracker.

Now let me tell you a little about D.K. D.K was a well-known underworld figure from the 80s and 90s, he was restricted from entering Kings Cross because of conditions put upon him by the courts. He was a very violent man and not many people crossed him and lived, so he wasn't able to look after his runners himself who were making over sixty thousand dollars per shift for him, so he offered me the gig. I would make about $10,000 a week just for being on call and dropping off the money to DK every morning. One year later, I would be in a Mexican standoff with DK after going to one of his dealers houses to collect a dept for another friend of mine, (since the dealer is under the protection of DK that meant I could not collect a debt for another), it could have gone either way that day but lucky for me DK was willing to negotiate, as we both held our guns under our coats with our finger on the trigger. DK called the guy I was collecting for and worked out a deal. I was relieved to walk away from that one. Many years later DK would be assassinated by his own boys.

Now let's get back on track.

Handling these two separate gigs earned me a lot of dough and I had plenty of time to spend it. Friends and associates would come to the Cross to visit me and I would host them impressively by showing them a part of Sydney that only a few of them experienced. If my visitors were from the street like me, I would take them to the most pleasurable parts of town – the clubs, restaurants, even casinos. But if my visitors were blue collar, there are also places for people like them. The Cross has a lot of cool spots for tourism. It's a town for all. No matter who you are, the Cross has a way of making you feel special.

You see, there was the Cross that punters would experience and then there was the Cross that the hustlers made a living from. It depends on which side of Cross you choose to be. The truth is that the Cross offers a variety of experiences that even native inhabitants are never tired of. The town seems to have a mind of its own; and that's probably why a lot of people living in the Cross are so prosperous whether they deal in illegal businesses or otherwise. The Cross is like Jesus Christ that treats both sinners and saints equally. Do not get me wrong, however; if your trade thrives in the underworld, do not draw unnecessary attention to yourself.

Permit me to retrace a few steps so that I can explain what I mean when I describe Fatty as my underworld uncle. I had two different families: my birth family which didn't have any criminal record because they didn't have a criminal among them – except me, of course. You are free to call me the family's metaphorical black sheep. Then there's my underworld family which has nothing but a long list of criminal records because, obviously, there's no single law-abiding citizen. If there was, the family wouldn't thrive in the underworld in the first place. That being said, Fatty is my underworld uncle;

we are not remotely related by blood but we share a very strong bond. In fact, I know more about Fatty than any of my real family members whom I had forsaken long before they ostracised me. Don't get me wrong, I love my family but we live in two different worlds; they are more like strangers than blood relations. Since I had learnt to depend on myself, I maintained my lane clear of them; and they, too, seemed to not want to have anything to do with me. They didn't believe they were better than the people I chose to associate with, they just wanted the best for me, which was their lifestyle not mine.

At this time of my life, I was living it up, catching up on the thrills of the Cross that I had been missing out on the last 12 months when I suddenly chose to be stupid. My underworld family must have believed a nut had gone loose in my head. The happiness in them was evident when I returned 'home' to them. I was in my prime and I planned to enjoy as much as I could; I wasn't going to allow any woman to hold me down again or try to change my orientation. The streets had done me more favour than I deserved – I swore loyalty to the streets.

One weekend when I was hanging around the main strip, I ran into an old friend from the Western suburbs. He was out with a couple of guys I had seen before but not close to them. I was introduced to them and that was how I met Bear who turned out to be the senior member of the Rebels motorcycle club. At the time I met him, Bear was on bail on the charge of murder; and the judge had explicitly put some hard conditions on his bail; the major condition was that Bear wasn't allowed to associate with other members of the Rebels or go to any of the club houses, so he started spending his time in the Cross.

At the beginning, I didn't know the gravity of his crime. The only thing I knew was that I didn't really care about the motorcycle club. I had never really fancied Bikies. To me, they were nothing but a bunch of huge thugs with tattoos, rings and bandanas. I never cared for the fact that they always moved around in numbers. I knew a lot about them, yet I didn't know much about them, so I didn't really spend much time with them before I met Bear. Actually, Bear gave me a different impression about Bikies. When I started partying with Bear, I began to see Bikies in a different light. They were actually good people – at least the majority of them. They are not really as violent as their appearance might suggest; they were just regular street guys. Bear and I were like two peas in a pod; we were basically inseparable. We did almost everything together. We would take plenty of drugs, drink huge amount of alcohol and have sex with plenty of women. I introduced Bear to most of my brothers in the Cross and he introduced me to a lot of his friends associated with bike clubs. The Turk was one of these people. He was with Bear every night I saw him in the Cross. The Turk was his driver at the time and I would get to know him very well later on but at this time it was just me and Bear, partying hard night after night and the Turk always there to look out for us.

The most impressive thing about Bear is his ability to hold his liquor. He could party as hard as anyone I knew, and never for once did I ever catch him fall off the wagon. He never lost control of himself, no matter how hard he drank, or the quantity of drugs he took. It was incredible the way he could maintain his stamina with everything. While I would be drunk enough to pass out, Bear would not even have a slur in his speech; he was always nimble both physically and mentally – and alert too. In fact, I often felt a lot at ease whenever Bear was around me. I could easily lose myself in his presence knowing that he had my back. I respected him a lot for this, so we spent a lot of time together. It was Bear who let me know that I was already living the life of the Bikies, the only difference was that I lived mine alone while the Bikies lived theirs together. I thought deeply about that and eventually agreed that he was right. There wasn't really much different between me and the Bikies if you take away the motorcycles and the peculiar sartorial representation. I could easily blend with them if I joined them.

Bear and I would occasionally spent time in Dancers. Dancers was one of my favourite places because it was on the end of the strip and it offered me a sense of security. The doorman at Dancers was a good friend of mine. He was called Jacko. He was six foot tall, weighed 120kg and had a face just as mean as his right hook. Jacko's right hand should be registered as a lethal weapon. Although Jacko had a license to carry a concealed weapon, he hardly used it. Instead, he would use his right fist to restore order. I had seen him in action more than once and none of those moments was a pretty sight. One that stood out to me was when a black guy, a lot bigger than Jacko tried to attack him. I can't recall the cause of the fight then, but I can still vividly recall how Jacko had carried himself that night.

The huge guy had come rushing towards Jacko. I could see that he was aiming to ram his huge body through Jacko and put him on his back where he meant to overpower him and rain blows down on him. He obviously wanted to show everyone around that he was a tough chap who believed he could take on Jacko because of his size. But Jacko was a lot more experienced; he wasn't phased as the huge guy rushed toward him like a bull. Before the clash, I noticed that Jacko's right fist was clenched; that was the only hand prepared for the fight. Then just as the huge guy was about to pummel him, Jacko threw a swift uppercut that caught the attacker below the jaw. As huge as he was, the impact of the blow sent him reeling backward a few steps before he crashed against a plastic table. He remained still on the floor; his lights had gone out. It was about five minutes when he came to. When he woke up, no one told him what had happened – he already knew. He simply picked himself up and walked away. The huge man was never seen again at Dancers. Rumours had it that he packed his things and left the Cross in shame. He obviously couldn't stand the humiliation; but he was not the only person Jacko had knocked out in that manner.

Jacko and I were relatively close. His weapon of choice was a 9mm Brownie that he only made use of when the situation absolutely demanded it. Whenever I brought any of my friends and associates to Dancers, knowing Jacko was around would give an extra peace of mind. If anything were ever to happen and I had to dispose of my weapon, I could always count on Jacko to have my back. You see, Jacko is licensed to possess a firearm, I am not.

So, whenever there was a raid by the police or something, Jacko was always ready to collect my piece and help me secure it until it was safe for me to have it back. As far as I know, I was the only person in Dancers Jacko chose to do this favour. Hell, I was the only one carrying a piece he would allow past the entrance. We share a mutual respect; I guess he respected me for the way I always carried myself. I didn't go to Dancers looking for trouble or anything of that sort, and I was capable of taking care of myself in case of any trouble. You can say Jacko was one of the reasons I enjoyed going to Dancers and Dancers was where I was going to meet my future wife, Jane, a few months later.

On this particular night, Bear and I were at Dancers drinking laughing and indulging. We were there for many hours throughout the night; and when sunrise was approaching, we went to the main strip so that I could check on the runners and know what they were up to. I did this every day. I needed to keep tabs on them so that they won't go astray. Then as we were walking past one of the strip clubs, Bear recognised someone he wanted to introduce to me. His name was Milperra, and that was the first time meeting him. If you know about the Milperra massacre of 1984, you will understand why this guy was named Milperra. He was one of the Bandidos during the shootout between rival Bikie club members. That shootout is popularly known as Father's Day Massacre that claimed seven lives and left almost thirty other people seriously injured. Fifteen years had passed since the shootout at Milperra and this guy was one of the last to get out of jail. At the time Bear introduced him to me, I didn't really know what to make of him. Was he dangerous? Could he be reasonable? What had the years he had spent in jail done to his personality? A lot of questions were going through my head as we shook hands.

Well, as soon as we were introduced, we went out for a drink and had some lines. For some reasons, Bear must have thought Milperra and I would be tight or something but unfortunately, Milperra and I didn't click. There was just something about him that didn't go along with my spirit. My guts told me there was something amiss somewhere – something was not right but I couldn't put my mind to it. The more I tried to figure it out, the more it eluded me. I know myself; whenever I had this kind of energy with someone, I always immediately dismissed the person and I would create as much distance between us as possible. I was having that kind of feeling with Milperra, but I kept dismissing it, hoping that I was wrong. Perhaps I was expecting to be convinced that I was only being paranoid. So, I pushed my suspicions aside and continued to show him the same amount of respect I always bestowed on anyone I would drink with. I chose the people I drink with carefully. To me, drinking is a kind of a sacred thing to do, and I would rather drink with my buddies rather than with total strangers; otherwise, I'd rather drink alone, or not at all. So, Milperra and I had a couple of drinks and we chatted occasionally. He told me stuff about the massacre that I already knew myself, but I pretended to show interest in what he had to say.

Bear and I began to roll together more often, and I started going to club houses with him; but we didn't visit any Rebel club house because Bear was still under restriction by his bail conditions. But besides the Rebel clubs, we would go to the 61, the Nomads, the Wolf's even the Bandidos where a lot of his buddies frequented. Bear was quite popular among the Bandidos, and indeed I learnt a thing or two from him. Bear and I were close enough to be friends for I can say that we had a few things in common. We basically scouted all the clubs. The only clubs we didn't drink in at the time were the Angels. At a time, Bear and I seemed inseparable; if you wanted to locate me you had to find the whereabouts of Bear. And because of Bear, I got to meet a lot of other good people. We were just cruising and chilling. A few brief business opportunities would crop up and we would take advantage but we were basically drink buddies. Having drinks without Bear to drink with me was something I never liked. It seemed like with Bear around the drinks tasted a lot better; and like I already said, Bear knew how to party hard; he was the life of most of the club houses.

After a few months, Bear's murder charges were dropped so he was able to visit the Rebel club house in Bringelly. From the beginning, Bear had wanted me to join the Rebels but I had no interest in that; being a Rebel wasn't really my cup of tea at the time. However, I admit that the lifestyle in the Bringelly club house was cool and all the members I met were loveable. They all seemed to like me. As I met them, I felt that Bear had most probably told these people about me. I didn't know what he must have told them but whatever it was, I was sure Bear had laced his narrative with a little bit of hyperbole. But at the back of my mind, I knew everything was bordering on Bear's attempt to recruit me into the Rebel, which I had resisted so far.

If I would join the Rebels, apparently, I would have to start as a Nom. A Nom is someone who starts off to becoming a full pledged member of the Rebel motorcycle club. Such a person would do odd jobs for the members and work at the club houses – things I didn't care to do. To me, being a Nom was not different from being the servants of these people; and it would take the person a year to serve them before finally being nominated to become a member. The idea of me working behind the bar and cleaning up after days of partying and being at the call of any member at any time for at least 12 months did not appeal to me. I wasn't cut out for that kind of lifestyle for I knew I would always have problems with the members; if one member ever got too drunk while I was serving him, things might get ugly between us. I have a very low threshold for bullshit. People who didn't know how to handle themselves whenever they were drunk often acted silly, and I would have none of that. That's just me; I wasn't being arrogant or anything, but a man has got to set standards for himself. When you allow every Dick and Harry to walk over you, they will be glad to turn you into a foot mat. And as soon as you are useless, they will toss you away like garbage. If you want people to respect you, do not only treat people with respect, you must also treat yourself with respect. It is how you see yourself that people will see you. Of course, people will try your patience, they will attempt to ride you and stretch you to the breaking point. The more you permit them to use you as they like, the more you lose your identity. In the end you will end up hating yourself.

One day Bear told me they had just negotiated a deal with a small bike club in Taren Point near Cronulla to be patched over. That consists of the boys from Taren Point handing in their colours to the Rebel's, and everything else that identified them as members of another bike club. In doing that, the Rebels would give them the front patch that goes on the front of their vests, this identifies them as patch members or Noms of the Rebels motor cycle club. They would have to serve as probationary members for 6 months, and if they passed, they would get their full colours.

Bear's intention was that I would Nom up with him and he would place me in Taren Point for six months and by the time the Taren Point boys got their colours. Bear would have a site in the city for a city chapter that he had picked. I kept letting Bear know that I wasn't interested in becoming a Nom, but he would not hear of it; he was very persistent. Bear wasn't a man who would give up easily. If I could join the members without becoming a Nom, Bear would have made that happen without thinking twice, but it was not possible. I would have to be a nom first. Bear obviously wanted me in the club and he would not accept my refusal.

"It's just for six months," he would always tell me. "In no time you will become a member. Trust me, you can do it."

Now the idea about me *noming* up with him didn't sound too bad, especially now that I knew what his plan was. I was going to Nom for six months with a couple of guys in my rank. I started thinking I could do it after all. To keep on, I should imagine that I was serving a 6-month term. Of course, it wouldn't be as bad as that, but I needed to imagine something like that to keep myself going through the process. And since I was doing it with people of the same rank with me, none of them would tell me what to do. After much persuasion from Bear, I finally accepted his deal. I chose to see my acceptance as a way of letting Bear know that I considered his friendship important enough to take something like that. And from the way his face lit up when I accepted the deed, I could see that he was indeed grateful.

I nommed up with two other guys; one was from Cronulla – a local that worked at the Shark League club as a bouncer – the other was the Turk. He had also been hanging around the club with Bear for many years but never made the move to join until now. That made me start to think that I wasn't the only person Bear had been trying to convince after all. I didn't know what to feel about this. I had no idea whether I should be relieved or disappointed. Whatever it was, I knew being a Nom wasn't going to be unbearable for me. And even if I found that I wasn't comfortable, I could easily walk away. As a matter of fact, I accepted simply because of Bear and I had no interest in becoming a member whatsoever. I liked my life as it was already. I was in charge of a couple of stripper and runners and money was coming in regularly. I was comfortable to a certain degree.

Perhaps another reason that made me accept the deal was curiosity. I wanted to know what it meant to be a member of the Rebels. What special privilege being a member offer? How would people see me in the society? How would I see myself? Was any of it worth it at all? All these and more were the questions that ran through my head as I agreed to nom up. It seemed to be a new form of experience. Well, I had six months to figure out what all the fuss was about being a Rebel. There must be a special reason why Bear wanted me so badly in the club. So many thoughts were swimming in my head but none of them might be true, since most of the thoughts were ridiculous, to say the least. I nursed the thought that I was being recruited because of my connection's. Something was coming up in the club and they need people like me to be on their side. It could be a move to expand. The more I thought about it, the deeper I went into the ridiculous rabbit hole. All I could think was that war was coming – just like the Milperra Massacre. Indeed, my ignorance was pathetic. The club was just doing what all clubs did "expanding", it was like a family-owned company, the bigger the family got the more power and property the company accumulated.

2

TAREN POINT CLUB HOUSE

Club House Life

I stopped working in the Cross and moved to a two-storey house near Cronulla. It was a great sacrifice that I had to forsake my job for being a Nom. I sincerely prayed I wasn't going to regret my decision. However, whatever the case might be, I could still return to Cross if things didn't work out as I wanted in Cronulla. I could always count on Fatty to take me back. He had always been there for me; he was an uncle better than any other uncle I could ask for.

My apartment in Cronulla wasn't bad. The backyard had a swimming pool; although it would fill up with the tide because the house was right on the edge of Gunnamatta Bay, it was still pretty to have a pool. Besides that, I also had a boat shed that opened up to my own boat ramp; it was the perfect party house. It could contain as many people as I wanted. Since I loved having parties, I assumed the house would come in handy. I had chosen this house myself; I chose what suited my style. I figured if I was going to do what Bear wanted, I was going to do it my way. I would not be a Nom living the lifestyle of a goffer, or looking like one. I am a man of very high taste who likes doing things with style; so, I assumed I had to live up to my identity.

The first month of my nomship was a little slow for me, especially after just coming out of the Cross. It would take a little time for me to adjust to this new life. I was still feeling the effect of leaving my original life to this alien one. Adjustment would have been worse and I would have quit a long time ago but for Bear that was there for me. He guided me through most of the process. With him around, things were relatively easy. I was able to cope fine all thanks to him. Bear was the senior member in charge of 15 noms, 12 patched-over bikies and three new noms. And because Bear and I were close, I had a better edge than most of the other noms in the same rank with me.

After the first month we had the club house in Taren Point looking like a Rebels club house. It was an impressive transformation. We all brought our A-games to the table; all credits belonged to the noms – we all did an incredible job. Everyone excelled in their various assignments. By the time we were through rebuilding the club house, the bar was full and the dancers ready to entertain. With a job well-done, we were ready to official open the first party of the club. I guess, in a way, we wanted to impress the members about our achievement. So, the first party we had there was for all the members of the other Rebel in Sydney to meet these new members. We were focused; our goal was to get the colours. We all agreed to work together to achieve that goal for we all knew that if we didn't measure up at the end of our six months' probation period, we would not get the colour – which was the major reason why we were doing all this in the first place. I was inspired; I hated embarking on anything and end up failing in achieving my goal. I wasn't going to allow it to happen. With me, failure was not an option. I poured my mind to the project and set various things in place. I wasn't only doing it for me, I was also doing it for Bear, for I knew how important this was to him.

So here we were – the first party for the Taren Point club house as Rebels. The number of turnouts was beyond our expectation, and it was the first sign that we were on the right track with our project. It was imperative that we met up to expectation, for anything less would not earn us the colours. About one hundred members came from Bringelly and other surrounding chapters, and I could see that the majority of them were impressed by what we had achieved so far. The party started off like every other party I had been to at a Rebel club house – maximum velocity, full ball, flat out, all the members drinking, snorting white powder and smoking plenty of green weed. We did not only set up a party, but we also made a lot of substances available – our aim was to give all the members maximum satisfaction.

The music was blaring, and the strippers were doing their thing, many of these strippers came there because of me. And they rocked everyone's world; they were beautiful young girls with amazing racks and the body to die for. Even after the party at the club, I hosted another after-party party in my house. Here, everyone was allowed to run wild. The swimming pool was filled with people who assaulted the water with various nasty activities.

I had a great time but I watched myself. I drank in moderation and took one girl named Emily to my room. She was the first girl I would be with since I moved to Cronulla. Although Emily was a stripper, she was one with a plan for her life, unlike most of her colleagues. She was already running her Masters in one of the prestigious universities. She wasn't planning to be a stripper forever. She told me a little bit more about herself. She already had a boy but that was not going to stop her from pursuing her dream. Emily had her eyes on the big picture and she was working very hard to attain that.

We spent a lot of time together that night and I would only see her a few more times before I found out she had moved on one day to a large law firm in Melbourne. After that night we would hold many more parties at the club house in Taren point so all the members from all around Australia could meet us and make their own decision on whether or not this new chapter of the Rebels made the cut. On one of these particular nights, Campbelltown and the Bringelly chapter members were drinking at Taren Point, and at about midnight the National President (let's call him the Barg, short for Bargwa), called a snap meeting where he announced that we were going to ride into the Cross, have a couple of drinks and then break off from there so the members that had to be in another place the next morning could go from there and the rest of the members could go back to Taren Point club house or Bringelly club house. You see, even though attending staged events at club houses and going on runs was compulsory, staying to the end was not, many members had jobs and families to go to so as long as you showed up to an event, how long you stayed was up to you.

A few minutes after the call we all mounted our bikes in the car park out of the front of Taren Point club house, it was an amazing seen to behold, one minute every one's drinking laughing and running wild the next minute we are all organized in formation like a well-trained military unit. Barg and the National Vice President Brownie took off first, leading the pack, then member after member followed side by side forming two rows like a freight train on two tracks, it was an amazing seen. This was my first run in such a large pack. There were only 100 of us riding but once we took off in two rows it seemed like the line went for ever. The formation usually consists of the most senior members in front, noms in the middle and hung arounds in the back. As you ride in a pack, you cannot break up the formation, so when we go through an intersection or a set of traffic lights, usually 2 or 4 members will block either side of the street so the whole pack can cross in one go together. As soon as the whole pack can cross the members blocking the intersection will let the traffic through and quickly return to their position in the pack. You couldn't let the pack get broken up when riding in with so many numbers, it would be mayhem on the streets if half the pack stopped at the lights and the other half kept on going or even stopped on the other side of the lights until they turned green again. That would traffic jams and if they kept going the ones stuck at the lights would have to ride hard and fast waving through traffic to catch up and re-form. It's just not practical and the police also knew this, so when they knew we were going on a run and where we were going, they would block the streets for us giving us a clear run, it was an amazing feeling. On this particular run I rode beside the Turk with the rest of the Taren Point chapter in front of us and behind us. Over the last few months, I had become very close to the Turk and very protective of him. He seemed innocent to this life style and I felt as though I needed to protect him maybe it was because he didn't drink or take drugs, and every time he was asked to do something, he did it without question. I felt as though other members were taking advantage of him so I stayed close to him when I could. Don't get me wrong, the Turk could take care of himself but he was just too nice for his own good. Always willing to please everyone and I had met many people like the Turk in the Cross. I watched them get eaten up by the more street wise occupants and I never liked that, so I made it my personal mission to look out for the Turk. He was my brother now and I wouldn't let anyone use my brother. So, there we were side by side in a pack of 100 riding to the Cross. The Turk on his red soft-tail with ape hangers and me on a blue fat-boy which I had only purchased a few months before. I had never ridden a Harley before I purchased this one, I have always ridden Jap bikes like Suzuki's or Kawasaki's, these were fast performance bikes, Harleys were not, it took a bit of getting used to, but I did. I couldn't ride the Harley like the Jap bike but I learned to ride them to the best of their capabilities. You lift them on one wheel or lean them right down in a corner but you could drop the clutch and fish tail the back wheel from one end of a street to the other.

This was new to me, so I practiced it as much as I could. I ended up going through three new tyres before I had enough. Another trick I liked doing on a Harley was to put it on cruise control and stand up on the seat with my hands off the handle bars, it was like surfing a Harley.

So, there we were riding into the Cross, 100 bikes with the majority of the riders over 100kg with beards and tatts all over their bodies. We took up both sides of the main strip, dismounted and all the members started taking off in groups of two or three, to all different clubs on the strip. The boys made sure they didn't all go into the same club at once, scarring off the other patrons. All the noms stayed back to look after the bikes, that was their only duty that night. This was also the first time my brothers in the Cross saw me with the Rebel patch on. I hadn't told anyone in the Cross I was joining the club, but after all the time I was spending there with Bear I think they knew. I said hi and shook hands with the doormen closest to the row of bikes. I was looking after and had a short chat with them on how things have been going since I left. The doormen couldn't talk long because they were always trying to get people into the strip clubs. You see, they worked off a system where you get paid on how many people you can get in to the club, so I let them do their thing and sat on my bike while I joked around with the Turk.

It was around half an hour after we got to the Cross that the Cops stationed in the Cross decided to make their appearance. As expected, they started to harass us by booking all the bikes parked on the main strip. They were also taking down number plates and description of the bikes that annoyed us and as they got closer to me and Turk, I started to think of different things to try and fuck them in their duties. I don't know what got into me but I jumped on the fat boy, put my skull cap on and took off fish tailing the full length of the main strip. First, I hammered it towards the fountain on one end of the strip and then to the Coke sign at the other end. I did this a few times before the cops could run back to their station and jump into their cars to chase me down. It wasn't long before both ends of the strip were blocked. I was now running on instinct, I didn't even know what I was going to do until I did it, at least they stopped booking the members bikes, but the chase was on. I have taunted cops my whole life but that was with fast performance bikes, this was my first chase on a Harley that performed like a boat or a caravan. However, I rode as fast as the motorcycle could possibly go, but I wasn't eluding my pursuers much, they were gaining considerably on me. It was only a matter of time before they caught up with me and ultimately arrested me. I had to make use of all my wits, my skills and in this case, it didn't involve Harley surfing, for what help would that be in my pursuit for escape? I had to use my brain effectively at this point.

The cops tried to block me under the Coke sign at first, but I managed to manoeuvre the Fat-boy past them, much to their surprise they must have been fuming with anger because I kept slipping away from them like an eel. In the teeth of danger, someone could tend to damn all rules and just try to survive. Knowing the problem, I had just invited upon myself, I gave my bike all it had and more; it was like I was floating; I didn't care about anything anymore at this stage the adrenaline was high. I had to save myself. I was running red lights, flying through intersections and scrapping the running board on the sides of the bike where you put your feet on at every corner. Again, the silence of the night worked in my favour. I cut through various corners and tried to shake them off, but the cops were equally determined.

Suddenly an idea crept into my thick head and I loved it. I quickly headed back towards Taren Point. My plan was to arrive at the club house with a considerable space between me and the pursuers. I would drop the security fence on them as I pass through and they would have a hard time getting in. It would be great advantage for me if they didn't see me pass through the fence because it would have given me enough time to take my vest off and join the others as if I had been there the whole time. If they came around, they would not discover shit. Thankfully, my Harley was not yet booked by the cops so there was no way they would be able to recognise it among the dozens of other motorcycles that would be parked there. And I was pretty sure that none of them saw my face because I was wearing my helmet all through the moment the bikes were being booked. It was a brilliant plan. If I could successfully carry it out, I would be bragging for a long time.

I was counting on the other noms looking after the club house to back me against the cops; and of course, they would as it was an unwritten code in the streets. The police are never your friend; do not betray your real friends for them, it's not worth it. Everything should go according to plan. As I was nearing Taren Point, I felt a surge of hope as there was now a noticeable distance between me and them. Unfortunately, with all the plans I had laid down, what I didn't anticipate was the gates were already down and locked. There was no way for me to get in and I couldn't just break through the barrier. I was riding a bike, not driving a train. My heart sank as I saw before me that the gates were already down. I looked behind me, but the pursuers were not in sight yet, but I could hear the faint sound of their sirens. The sound was getting louder and louder with each passing second.

I calculated that I had about ten seconds between me and the highway patrol before I got to the club house. At this point, every second was critical. I quickly dismounted from my bike and tried to get through the gates. They were not only brought down; they were also firmly locked. I was sunk. Then I did the only thing I could do next. I yelled at the top of my voice calling on the other noms at the other side to come and open up. They seemed to have heard me but they were too slow to react. I was calling on them to hurry up, time was running out. I only had a few seconds before the car appeared. It was either the gates were opened now or there was no point anymore. I was sweating profusely as I waited for the men to act.

But they responded too late. Two cop cars came to a screeching stop in front of the driveway and the men jumped out with their weapons drawn. I was cornered; there was nowhere else for me to go anymore. I was at my wits' end. There was no doubt that I would be arrested now. Nothing could save me at this moment. Those noms had acted too slow; I would have escaped if they had not been so damn sluggish.

"Stop right there!" one of the cops screamed at me as they carefully approached me.

"Put your arms behind your head," the other ordered sharply – the whole familiar shenanigan.

I didn't do as I was told; at least not immediately. All I could think of at that moment was to protect the patch, so I took off my vest and passed it to the nom through the fence. As soon as I passed the vest across the cops jumped me, but the deed had already been done; there was no way they could get back the vest.

They pinned me to the floor and cuffed my hands behind me.

"What are you doing?" I said as they worked on me. "I haven't done anything wrong." I continued to lie but the cops were not responding – they may as well have been deaf. A soon as my wrists were successfully manacled, the cops lifted me to my feet and took me to their car. Of course, I denied that I was riding any bike even though it was clear that I was; my falsehood didn't stop them from arresting me.

At the station, I refused to give them my name; and by 6 a.m. I was still in the dock waiting for my prints and mug shot so they could make a proper ID on me. That way they could charge me and give me a court notice. But I wanted to make things as hard for them as possible even though all they wanted was to find out who I was so they could charge me and give me bail. So, there I was sitting in the dock and waiting for my fingerprints to come back. I still hadn't been properly searched at this point so I thought I better check my pockets just to make sure I didn't have anything in them I shouldn't have.

Occasionally, I would carry a few rolls of weed in my pocket. Sometimes it would be coke or some other drugs; and if any of them was caught on my person it would spell serious trouble for me. On dipping my hands into my pockets, I discovered that I had two satchels containing two grams of coke. My heart first skipped a beat. I didn't have to bring them out to know what they were. As soon as I felt them, I quickly put them both in my mouth and started chewing on them. I made sure none of the cops noticed what I was doing even though I was right in front of the duty officer and all the other cops walking past me. I chewed those two satchels of coke until it was all gone in five minutes, and none of the officers suspected anything. When I felt my brows, they were damp with sweat. That was a close one. If any of the satchels had been found on me, I would be totally sunk. I was just lucky that the thought to check my pockets occurred to me at the right moment.

The gravity of what I was doing didn't occur to me at the time I was doing it. I was desperate to get rid of any evidence on me, so I didn't think twice before chewing the satchels. After a while, the coke started taking effect on me. I shouldn't have taken that much. I knew, but I had no choice. Besides, at that desperate moment, my action was a spur-of-the-moment – safety first, whichever way it came. I started smiling. It was the duty officer that first noticed the change in my personality. He regarded me with a strange expression.

"Are you okay?" he asked in a concerned manner.

My smile broadened and I nodded vigorously.

"You look weird," he stated suspiciously.

I realised that I must be careful. If I acted too weird, he might discover that I was high. I shouldn't attract that kind of trouble to myself; I was already in, enough for one day. I tried to act cool but it was not easy; you know, it's hard fighting the high. Fortunately for me, I was not suspected of drugs; I think they believed I had multiple personalities as I was engaging with free conversation with the cops and even joking around with them. I was a different person. The coke made me unusually happy; I had no idea about the reason for my happiness but I felt I had no problem in the world whatsoever. I was on top of the world – elated for no reason. In my strange mine, I ended up telling them my full name and address – the same information I had sworn to never give them. Well, I guess I couldn't eat my coke and still have it, if you understand what I mean. I was singing like a parrot; I was sure that if they had asked about all the crimes I had committed in the past. I would narrate everything without thinking twice. Surprisingly, however, none of them suspected anything amiss about me, considering my initial taciturn attitude when I was brought in.

Perhaps because of my cooperation, and the fact that I entertained them with my jokes, I was allowed to make a call to the club house. Of course, I knew that it was my fundamental human right to make a call, but some reason I suspected that they wouldn't allow me if they didn't want me to. Perhaps it was the effect of the drugs that was making me imagine all these. I spoke with one of the noms in the club house and told him to bring my license to the station so the cops could process me. As soon as that was done, I went back to Taren Point for three days and nights of partying with hardcore members that stayed behind after the ride that weekend.

And for the next five months, there would be many more weekends like that; it was routine. Taren Point chapter kept a low profile during the probation period. We would have a meeting once a week (we called it church meeting) and open the bar every Saturday for the purpose of raising money for the chapter. You must remember now that these Taren Point boys already had a ranking structure: there was Chief – he was presiding over all those boys, just like the chief of a town or community would do – then there was his Vice-President, Sergeant-of-Arms, and the Treasurer. As a matter of fact, the organization was basically a community of its own, with its peculiar rules of law. I, and the two other noms, was at the bottom of that ranking structure. We were the unranked newbies who would have to work for the ranked members. Every now and then I had to remind them that they didn't have their colours yet, which was the main goal. It's my job to make sure none of us lose any focus – getting the colours was the goal and we must achieve it. I would not be a part of failure.

Chief decided to make up a schedule so everyone had time behind the bar and doing all the other things noms had to do, such as looking after the bikes on meeting nights and party nights, and also cleaning up after a big weekend. These were basically all the things I hated about being a nom. It was a humiliating task, and I didn't know how long I was going to endure it. But every time, I still found myself putting the good of the chapter first before every other thing. But still, it was always very annoying whenever I had to wait and watch bikes while the other members had meetings or party hard. It was always like I was being denied my rights. If the task had only been watching over the bikes it would have been a lot less humiliating to endure, but I had to clean up after them. It was incredibly annoying. Every time I did it, I felt I was being a gross disappointment to myself. Besides the fact that the job was an embarrassing one, it had no excitement, except on some very few occasions when I had to put some of the rude members in their places. I remember once knocking a member across the jaw for talking out of school. My fellow noms had thought I had gone crazy; to them, it was unheard of for a nom to attack a member. Everyone, including me, had thought I would be kicked out for what I did; but surprisingly I wasn't. I suspected that Bear must have pulled some strings or something. But since that moment, I had always been respected, even by the hierarchy. It seemed like they were making sure I would have no reason to raise my fist on any one of them. One way or another, a man must demand his respect.

I didn't always stress myself unnecessarily in anyway if it could be avoided. Whenever it was my turn to do the bar, I would hire topless waitresses to serve the drinks for me while I sat back and partied with visiting members and locals. The waitresses were always ready to do my bidding. Some of them I didn't even have to pay as long as they had the opportunity of being part of the parties, they were good. Some of them were ready to go beyond just serving drinks; they were there to make the visitors even more comfortable. That was where most of them made their money; it was a lot more than whatever I was willing to pay them. Because I knew a lot of strippers, the party was never short of waitresses willing to go topless. At a point, my system became the envy of my fellow noms who didn't have the resources to hire waitresses like I always did. They all wished they could do like me but they didn't have the money or the connection. So, I became the subject of jealousy. While they were working hard, I chose to work smart with my available resources.

When it was time for me to clean up the club house after the party, I would also hire a professional cleaner. I had enough money to spend; I had made quite a lot in my days of working with Fatty, and some other side hustles. The only thing I couldn't hire people to do, the only thing that required that I must do myself was looking after the bikes. If I could hire people to do it, I would have gladly put someone else in my place, but it was not possible – something like that wasn't allowed. But I still made good use of that; I always tend to see opportunities where there seems to be none. By watching over the bikes, I had the good chance to talk to long-time members and really get to know them without the sound of music blaring in the background. They told me a lot of stuff that, ordinarily, a mere nom like me was not supposed to know. I got into the confidence of a lot of them. They all seemed pretty cool and polite; I felt like they were already seeing me as a part of them.

One of these nights, Chief was out the front with me trying to explain how all his members from the club were resenting me because I wasn't putting in the hard work they were.

"They believe you're cutting corners," he told me.

I frowned. I didn't immediately understand what he was talking about. "Cutting corners? What do you mean, Chief?"

"Hiring topless waitresses, using cleaners, making others do your jobs for you – do all these rings a bell?"

"But I'm getting the work done, aren't I?" I asked back, "Actually, I'm getting things done more efficiently than any other person."

Chief nodded. "Yes, you are."

"I don't see why anyone would have any problem with my style. If the boys are smart enough, they are free to do the same."

I admit, I said this as a form of mockery because I knew that they couldn't afford to do what I was doing. Doing something like that cost money but none of them had that much to spare.

He seemed to think about what I said, then he remarked, "I guess you're right."

"Remember, these guys are Rebels now. They are no longer some backyard bikie club. They had to step up in their game" Chief continued.

"But still, I think you should occasionally take responsibility."

"What do you mean by that, Chief?"

"Once in a while, you should do the bar yourself whenever it's your turn. Of course, you can employ others occasionally but don't make the habit permanent, it's not sitting well with a lot of people. And if it's time to clean up, try to do it yourself too; it won't make the other members feel like they were lesser than you, or anything of that sort. I hope you understand what I'm talking about."

I nodded in understanding. But I wasn't willing to take any of his advice. I would be damned before I allowed myself to clean up after anyone or sit behind the bar and serve people unless I wanted to. As I was about to make my case further before him, I noticed one of the locals that had been drinking at our club house all that night pissing on Chief's bike. But I didn't say anything immediately because Chief went on trying to tell me other things to do to fit in with the boys instead of telling them what was expected of them now that they were about to become full members of the biggest bike club in Australia. On a normal circumstance, I would have stepped towards the guy and set him straight, but I chose to not really interfere in this; I remained seated on my bike and continued listening to Chief for a few more seconds as he continued his unending spiel. Plus, Chief had a big swastika symbol painted on both sides of his tank. I never liked that sort of shit so I let the guy get to the shake before I casually said to Chief, "I think that guy is pissing on your bike." It was a great opportunity to take his attention away from the issue of me and the boys. I expected him to react furiously to seeing someone take a piss on his bike. It was a sign of disrespect.

Chief turned to have a look and then turned back to me. "It's just Jonesy."

"But he's pissing on your bike."

"He's obviously drunk," he replied casually.

"I don't give a fuck who he is or if he's drunk. That guy is pissing on your bike; you've got to do something. Should I get rid of him?"

Chief looked over again, then he turned to me and said, "Don't worry, I'll take care of it."

He walked up to his bike and had a look, bent over and had a better look, and that's when I heard him yell out "Jonesy!" he had obviously noticed that Jonesy had pissed on his tank. He was screaming hard at the guy now. I didn't join them. I remained seated on my bike and watched everything unfold and quietly smiled from within me. Finally, what I wanted had been achieved; something relatively more serious had sufficed. Chief was fuming in anger as he continued to scream into the drunk guy's face. The recipient didn't even seem to feel much qualm about what he had just done.

Chief called his Sergeant-of-Arms, Troy, and relayed to him the abomination that had just happened. The Sergeant had been called simply because he was a friend of Jonesy's; so, he was automatically responsible for what his friend had done. Now because of what had happened, the Sergeant-of-Arms and Jonesy would have a fight – Jonesy had pissed on the Chief's bike, so he would have to redeem himself by having a go. It was interesting that he would have to fight his friend. Knowing that Jonesy was drunk, I expected that the fight would be over in five seconds – Troy was the Sergeant-of-Arms, a position given to the hardest and toughest member. Besides, Troy looked bigger and more experienced than Jonesy; I expected the fight to be a walk in the park for Troy since he should know how to use his fist well, considering his position, and the fact that Jonesy was not in his right state of mind. A little child should easily defeat Jonesy in this kind of fight. Troy should knock him out in five seconds.

But boy was I wrong. The fight was the most pathetic I had ever seen. There seemed to be no difference between the two fighters. Jonesy was swinging and missing, Troy was swinging and missing. At first, I thought the two were only pretending to fight, that they didn't want to hit each other because they were friends, but I was wrong – the two were simply pathetic. The fight went on for an incredible three minutes and neither had landed any serious punch on the other. I could see that Troy was beginning to run out of air. If I didn't do something fast it would have been a very big embarrassment for these boys; they were fighting like little kittens scared of each other. To quell the impending disgrace, I stepped in. I grabbed Jonesy by the neck with my left, ready to knock him out with my right. Troy, still trying to catch his breath, placed his hand on my shoulder and said:

"No! It's okay; he had a go; I don't think he's going to do that again."

I was dumbfounded; but after that Chief never complained to me again.

Paintball Weekend

The next weekend was when Chief and the other 11 probationary members were to get the vote by all other members to see if they get colours; so Chief had organized a big weekend to try and show all the old school members he had something new to bring to the table. Chief was heavily into paintball, unlike now, paintball games were new in those days and were just gaining popularity, so Chief organized Taren Point, Bringelly and Campbelltown chapters for a game of paintball. I remember I was looking forward to that weekend because I had never tried paintball before and from what I had learned about it, it was just like war games, and boy will be boys. In the past, I spent many weekends hunting and going through real training for this sort of thing with old Bob, (I will tell you about him soon), but never with so many people.

So, the weekend was set, Chief wanted to make it a family event so the members were asked to bring their wives or girlfriends if they wanted, a barbeque was organized with plenty of drinks and food, it was a well-organized event.

So, on the weekend of the paintball event, Campbelltown and Bringelly chapters rode off from Bringelly club at about 9 a.m. and as usual many members were continuing from the night before. They all rode down from the west to Taren Point where they all dismounted and had a few drinks while Chief gave instructions to all the noms driving the support vehicles. I was at the bar talking to a few of the Campbelltown and Bringelly members that I had gotten to know very well, most of them through Bear. I had clicked with these guys because of the way they did things, there was no halfway with these boys, it was always to the most extreme, whether it was drinking, riding or fighting, they did it well, they were brave, focused and goal oriented; they shared the same ideology as me. This was also the weekend I was to meet Rebel Rick for the first time; Rebel Rick was a legend in the club. I had always heard stories about him from other members but I thought that they were always stretching the truth a bit, boy was I wrong.

Rebel Rick was a legend in the club. He was feared and respected all around; Rebel rick had the reputation of making noms think twice about the lifestyle they had chosen; and according to what I heard, no one would dare say NO to Rick. When I met Rick, he had just gotten out of jail for armed robbery and he was looking to catch up on lost time. I didn't know how long he spent behind bars but from the look of things it seemed like it wasn't entirely a short time. When I finally met Rick, I expected someone who exuded power like I had often heard about him, but I was wrong, he was quiet, polite and funny, not at all what I expected, but first impressions aren't always correct.

So, there we were, all details taken care of and all on our bikes ready to go. Chief was running this show, so he took the scenic route towards the paintball course. When we got there, the noms set up everything and the members started doing their thing, having a good time and straight away, they didn't waste any time on frivolities. As soon as the president of the Campbelltown chapter stepped on the course, (this is one of the members I mentioned before as never doing things halfway) the game was on!

The atmosphere suddenly changed and everyone was in the spirit of competition. Cheering and shouting ensued among the spectators as they encouraged their teams. I stood there watching with interest not because one of my favourite guys was playing the game, but the game had not really started. Chief and the officials from the course were trying to explain the rules to the members. What a big mistake. As they were passing out the safety equipment

– masks, goggles, chest plates and overalls – Simon, the Campbelltown President, started shooting them with a fully automatic paintball gun. As they scurried away trying to protest, a few of the members started laughing, so Simon turned his attention to them, shooting them in the legs and torso. Immediately, everyone started reaching for their weapons. They filled their weapons with paintballs and started shooting at anyone in sight. It was like a warfront; hilarious and serious at the same time. People were screaming at each other and barking orders. Anyone who didn't know better would think this was an ambush. I was having a really good time; it had been a while since I laughed as hard as I was in the moment. Imagine 20 to 30 members with paintball machine guns in a course made out to resemble a jungle. I felt at home among the members; it seemed like that was where I belonged as I ran around with my own gun and shooting everyone I met. At this point, no one had any ally; you had to shoot anyone you found, and if you were shot, you were out of the game. I tried as much as possible to prevent myself from being shot. There was a slight rush of adrenaline as I ran around; I felt like Rambo, jumping and ducking paintballs. While some of us were shooting at one another, there were some members and families who didn't care to join in the game; they were having fun just drinking and laughing at the ones playing the game; and there was a net separating them from the players. So, there was no chance that someone who had no regard to rules could target them.

In the course, no one wore masks or goggles; the only thing they did was take off their colours so no paint would get on them. Besides that, they were basically exposed to whatever stains from the paints, and they didn't seem to mind. But a couple of them still had their sunglasses on which was not a great idea, because they had their heads targeted by the ones who didn't wear any sunglasses. It was indeed a sight to behold. All through the day members left the course to occasionally eat, drink and take drugs, but there was still always someone on the course at all times playing the game. Even the Barg took hold of two guns and came out shooting. As he was shooting no one shot back at him. I found it weird; this was only a game; we were meant to have a good time with one another. Why would they not shoot at him? I never understood why. I suspected that people didn't want to offend him or something. It was incredibly silly to even imagine. Anyway, the game continued.

And as the day went on, I began to get a little bit fed up with Rick; he seemed to be terrorizing all the noms and shooting them down. He got me twice with the paintball. He seemed to be targeting only me and the noms, as if he had a personal vendetta against us. I had anticipated that someone would deserve what I made the night before, but I didn't anticipate it would be a member with such a good reputation in the club, but I had to do what I had in mind.

In my early 20s I spent a lot of time with Bob, an ex-special forces soldier who served in Vietnam during the war and later all around the world as a security adviser. I would go out shooting with him every weekend for one and a half years at a property near Goulburn. He was to teach me things that would shape me into the man I am today. It wasn't that I was looking forward to joining the Marines or something, but I appreciate a few nuggets of experience from him, for I knew that whatever I learnt from Bob would eventually come in handy. As a man, there were things I was expected to know, especially someone from the streets like me. Having military experience might place me in a better edge than some of my colleagues in the game. And so, one of the things I learnt from Bob was explosives – how to make them and how to effectively make use of them. It was a very interesting learning process; I had no idea how incredible it is to make explosives.

So, the night before the paintball weekend I made some mercury fulminate. This was a very simple but highly explosive powder made from mercury found in thermometers. You can break it down by using a certain acid and then drying the powder left behind. This is the same powder you use in a detonator to detonate a secondary explosive. It wasn't an idea someone could just easily come up with. Sure, chemists might be able to understand the components; but you see, for people like me, it was a privileged knowledge. It was a dangerous substance, and if not carefully carried out might result in a catastrophic and premature explosion, which could easily kill the person trying to produce it. Explosives of that kind should be processed in a controlled environment, and there must be adequate precautions. Anyway, without giving a damn about environmental precautions, I made two percussion grenades; that's basically a big bunger. Sometimes I wonder myself how I always did the things I did. I remember making the grenades without flinching about how it could kill me if I made any slight miscalculation of the powder. In a way, I considered myself a daredevil; I was willing to step into places where even Angels feared to tread. When I was done with making the explosives, I calmly packed them in a paper container with a 10 second fuse. I made the explosives with the same calmness and nonchalance as I would have made a sandwich. If the government had learnt about what I was doing in my little basement I would have been locked away in a place even God would not be able to break me out. At a point, I considered making explosives for profit. I could just make the grenades for crims and I would be paid huge sums of money. It was a good way of making cool hard cash; but when I weighed things, I realized that doing that would not be a good idea.

I quietly slipped away from the other noms when I saw Rick get back on the field. I didn't want him spraying me with paintballs anymore; his nonsense was beginning to get on my nerves and it wouldn't be right if I just lost it there at that time. We were all having a good time; I didn't want to ruin the moment. As I left, I ran down the dry creek bed running along the side of the course; no one could see me but I could see everyone on the course just by climbing up a bit on the bank of the creek. I had come here with the intention of getting back at Rick. If he knew how to play the game, I wanted to show him that I was a pro at playing games. I was willing to take it up a notch and take him by surprise. As soon as I saw where Rick was, I smiled and positioned myself. He wouldn't know what hit him. The thought alone brought a smile across my face. I brought out one of the two grenades I had kept in my bag, then I started taping about ten paintballs around it. I had no intention of causing fatality; it all depended on how I controlled my aim. If I threw it directly at Rick he would be hurt. I might not have liked some of Rick's methods of doing things but I didn't hate the guy – and, of course, I didn't want him hurt. When I had taped the paintballs on the grenade, I lit it up. I held it in my hands and counted until the last four seconds. I understood the danger of still holding on to it. The grenade could explode in my face and cause some damage, but I waited till the last four seconds before I threw it in Rick's direction. I measured my aim in a manner that it was a few yards away from the target. If it landed too close to him, Rick and everyone around him would be hurt. I didn't want that. As I threw the grenade, I quickly left my spot and ran back along the creek bed towards the spot I had entered from. I didn't want suspicion to fall on me. But I must have taken only about three long strides when I heard the grenade go off. It was louder than I had anticipated and more powerful – the sound was deafening. I admit, even for a moment, I thought I had created an irreparable damage. The explosion was so powerful that it disintegrated the paintballs. My intention was to splash the paintballs on Rick, but things went awry. Thankfully, I wasn't discovered to be the perpetrator of the explosion. It was later I learnt that Rick and the other members near him felt the shock wave and their ears were ringing for one hour after. I joined everyone and pretended to be in shock as the other. Members were running helter-skelter. Some produced their weapons and searched for any adversary. For a moment, it was a great pandemonium; I started blaming myself for doing what I did. I had no idea that my action would cause an effect of such magnitude. Perhaps I didn't aim it right; but I was honest with myself, that wasn't the reason. There was no way what I planned to do would have happened. I was lucky that there was no serious casualty.

I got away with that one, but I wasn't game enough to let the other one off; the first had done enough damage already. It was hard recovering from that one. Fortunately for me, no one knew it was me who did it except for Simon. He was the only person who knew, and he let me know he knew. There was only one way he must have known; he must have watched me slip away from the court and the other noms. He must have put two and two together from there. Hell, he might even have trailed me to my location to determine what I was up to. One way or another, Simon knew my secret. I had spent a lot of time with Simon in the past five weeks and he knew what I was like. Even without trailing me, Simon would know that I was the only person capable of doing something of such magnitude; he most probably knew me more than any other person there. He would always confront me with it but I always denied that it was me. No matter what I told him, Simon would not be fooled. But he never ratted me out to the others. If Omerta was a person it would be Simon. Whenever the issue about the explosion was raised, Simon would cast me a knowing look and smile, and I always smiled back. There was no use hiding it; his impression about me would not be changed. I feel that my action that time made Simon respect me even more. He didn't know it, but Simon earned my respect too for keeping silent about that issue. He had proved himself to me to be a trustworthy man.

When the day ended, we all rode to a pre-arranged destination and broke off from Campbelltown and Bringelly. The fun was obviously over. Campbelltown and Bringelly went back to their club houses, and we went back to Taren Point. And from there all the Taren Point boys broke off and went home. I went to my place after getting rid of the other grenade. I had no intention of taking something as dangerous as that home with me. I can't really remember how I got rid of it. I think I threw it into the river or buried it. I think it must have been the river.

It was Sunday night now; I didn't have any plans. I had a shower and looked at the two blood blisters Rick had given me. The spots were turning dark now. I didn't need to treat the sores; in a couple of days my skin would return to normal. Fingering the blisters, I smiled to myself knowing that I got even with him. For the rest of his life, he would not forget the sensation in his ears. It was just too bad that he wasn't aware that it was me who did it. But I had consolation knowing that he got slightly hurt. I felt bad for the other members whose ears had also rung like Rick's; they were innocent. Unlike Rick, they didn't deserve that, I guess that it was merely collateral damage. At least their situation wasn't anything serious. Maybe some other day I would have the chance to let Rick know that I wasn't someone he could just mess with. This time around I would make sure that he suffered the consequence of his action all alone. Sometimes you have got to put some people in their place, as they tend to stray occasionally.

Rick

Later on, that night, I was starting to doze. My body was aching from all the war games. I must have exerted myself more than I thought. I thought about taking painkillers but I was too tired to rise from the bed. I just wanted to lie there and sleep it off. By tomorrow morning, I would be as good as new. All I needed right now was good sleep, enough sleep. Then as I was about to crash, my phone rang. I groaned aloud. It couldn't have rung at a worse time. I lazily reached for it and pressed the green button. It was the noms from Bringelly. Earlier that day at the paintball ground they had told me how they hadn't slept since Friday.

They were complaining about Rick who had recruited all four Bringelly noms and he wouldn't let them go until he was finished with his drinks. And knowing Rick's reputation as an incurable dipsomaniac, that could have been another three days. And because the noms knew that too, and they also knew my reputation of going as hard and as long as any other member, they called me and asked for my help. They wanted me to deliver them from the hands of Rick. I felt very bad for them as they were so unlucky to be recruited by someone as mischief as Rick.

These boys were my brothers now. We had gone through so much together. I would take a bullet for them if the situation demanded it. And with my history, they didn't even need to ask for my help. I told them on phone that I would come and help them. Even though I was aching all around, I didn't hesitate to jump off my bed. I dressed up and took the painkillers I had initially decided against. My original plan was to drive up to Bringelly club house and see if I could convince Rick to come to the Cross with me which, of course, was highly unlikely. Trying to convince Rick to do anything was as hard as trying to persuade a Sphinx to smile. So, I jumped into my car and drove off. I was driving a replica 351 Shelby Cobra. It was a 2-seater convertible. The car was very sexy-looking but it wasn't practical. As a matter of fact, I hardly used it. I would only drive it when it was absolutely necessary, or when I wanted to show off. All in all, even as sexy and pretty as it was, the car wasn't really my favourite. It's a car you could only drive on good days because it had no roof. I didn't buy the car. A friend of mine gave it to me a few months before. He was hoping I would buy it off him. I would have bought it but I saw no point; it was just an average car as far as my taste went. However, I admit that it was fun driving it for a while. Whenever its owner was ready to take it back, I would return it with pleasure.

With the wind blowing my hair and giving me a bit of soothing feeling, I headed off towards Bringelly. It was a short but quiet drive. There were only a few cars on the highway. I arrived at my destination sometime after midnight and found Rick at the bar with three noms. I wasn't surprised. The bar was arguably Rick's most favourite place in the world. Anywhere he could have an abundance of booze, there would Rick tarry. Apparently, one of the four noms had enough and taken off. As soon as I got there and Rick saw me, his first words were: "Here we go. The replacement is here."

I smiled and approached them. I perched myself behind the bar and made a cup of coffee. Rick further made himself a line and finished his drink. I could see that

the three noms were happy to see me. Their savour had
come. Rick would only drink Jack Daniel and Coke so I
made Rick another drink. As we were talking generally, I
pulled out a bag of coke and offered Rick and the noms.
I had never seen Rick turn down an offer of coke. There
were two things in this world Rick would never say no
to – booze and drug. Women, he could easily do without
them. Food he could go for days without eating anything,
as long as he had his booze with him. While Rick accepted
the coke, the noms rejected it. They didn't want any
part of it, they just wanted to go home; they were tired.
Rick and I had a few lines each and I suggested we go
somewhere where more was happening. Now thinking
about it, I was sure the noms were disappointed. I had
come to save them from Rick but what I was doing didn't
sound anything like salvation, and it was rubbing wrongly
on them. But what I offered Rick was simply for their
benefits. I couldn't straight up just take them away from
Rick like that; things didn't work that way. Rick was a
powerful and respected member; I had to respect him.
The only thing I could do was bait him, which was what
I was doing. I knew the noms didn't approve of what I
was doing but I was sure it was going to pay off. Rick,
not knowing my intentions, took the bait straight away.
He jumped off his stool and said, "Yep, let's go. Everyone
mount up, we are going into the Cross."

I didn't imagine it was going to be so simple persuading
Rick to go to the Cross with me. It was like he had been
expecting it; perhaps it was the drinks taking control of
his rationality now. But I didn't want the noms to join us;
that would be against my plan, which was giving the noms

the freedom they wanted. So as soon as Rick spoke to the noms, I quickly cut in.

"Oh no, Rick. I want only you and me."

Rick stared at me and said, "What about these ones?"

The three noms exchanged glances. It was beginning to occur to them that I wanted to get them away from Rick. I could see the expression of delight on their faces.

"If it were me and you, we could get into any club. If we took these three with us, it's not going to look good for the business owners. Besides, we can easily pick-up women if it were just the two of us."

My last statement brought a smile to his face. After alcohol and drugs, the next item on Rick's favourite list was women. He turned to the three noms and said, "I hope you don't mind. You won't be able to come with us. You can go home now."

The noms started to rise from their seats. They looked totally relieved.

"Good night, Rick," they said as they filed out of the club house. They bade me good night too.

"Make sure you keep your phones on," Rick told them as they were leaving the club. "I may call you any one of you anytime soon." That was vintage Rick; he wasn't going to let them off easily. But I was going to make sure Rick wasn't going to disturb them. I would keep him so engage that he wouldn't have time to think about the poor noms.

Rick and I jumped into the Cobra. To be honest, I didn't want to do this. I was too tired from the war game. I just wanted to sleep; but I couldn't leave those poor boys at his mercy. Rick, being a 6-foot 120kg man, had to squeeze into the passenger's seat. It was hard getting him into the car; and after many attempts, he finally managed to get into the seat. On our way to town, I informed Rick that I couldn't park the car anywhere in the Cross. I suggested we drop the car off at my place first, then we would hitch a taxi from there. Rick frowned and reluctantly agreed. It was a strategy. If I had told him this before leaving Bringelly, he might have refused to come with me, and that would not be good for the noms. Even if he would come, he would make the other noms drive us; still, that would ultimately affect my plan.

When we arrived at my place, we didn't leave immediately; we had a few more lines as we waited for the taxi. As soon as the taxi arrived, we packed our shit and boarded it. The taxi took us straight to the Cross. The first club I took him to was one of my favourite clubs – Dancers. I was confident that he was going to have a very nice time in Dancers. I was right. Rick loved it; everything he wanted was provided for him. The waitresses were bringing drink after drink, and everything was on the house. I had made sure of that. Rick enjoyed free drinks as much as anyone else, and he was ordering exotic drinks. Even the girls treated him well; they made him feel like a king as they loved up on him. They loved his bag of magic white powder. The girls knew me, they were used to me giving them coke all the time which only lasted 30 or 40 minutes every line; and having Rick with an extra bag was nothing short of paradise for them. As a matter of fact, they were ready to go all out for him. They didn't realize that Rick was snorting speed, so these girls were peaking. At about 5am I took Rick to the main strip and we went from one club to the other. Rick was ready to try anything presented before him. We went from one club to the other until we ended up at the Kings Cross hotel. By that time, I was so worn out already that it was hard for me to move my legs. I consoled myself with the thought that I was able to come through for the three suffering noms. I hoped that someday when I needed their help, they would stand up for me too. Rick and I stayed at the hotel till eight o'clock the next morning. I didn't know whether Rick had some sleep or not, but the little I had was invigorating.

At one point we were drinking with two Bandidos and one of their noms, which they called Prospects. The two Bandidos were Sasha, the president of the Bandidos Pyrmont chapter, and Milperra. I knew Sasha from the Cross but I had dealings with him since the early 80s from my days in Cabramatta. Sasha was an absolute gentleman and I liked his way of doing things. He was a cool guy to be with. He had great respect for himself and others. He was one of the most honest people I knew; but I still had reservations about Milperra; I had a problem trusting him. Like I already mentioned, Milperra and I never clicked. We had different interests; there was no way I could be friends with him. I think even he knew that. We were not foes, of course; we were cool but our relationship never went further than a mere acquaintance. We could have a couple of drinks occasionally but that was it, nothing went further than that. I consider myself a good judge of character. And within the few moments I met Milperra, I decided that he didn't have the kind of character I would like to associate with. The prospect's name was Snake. He was a giant who looked very intimidating. As I stared at him, I wondered if I would be able to take him if a fight broke off between the two of us. From experience, I know size doesn't always matter. A smaller person with a good experience can easily beat an inexperienced giant – it could easily be the case of David and Goliath. But it is not all giants that are inexperienced. Huge people who really knew how to fight were always very formidable. And from studying Snake, I could tell that he could hold his own if there was a brawl, still, I wasn't sure that he could flatten me. He might be intimidating but I wasn't too worried.

Rick knew them all very well. His reputation went beyond just the Rebels; every club knew Rick. I later learnt that Snake only looked intimidating; he was a freaking dud. So, Rick and I drank with these three. At one point, Rick got Snake to piggyback him to the bar so he could get his drink. It was hilarious. It seemed to me like Rick was treating Snake like a personal assistant. And it was even funnier that the giant didn't decline. Eventually they all left and it was just Rick and myself again. Except for the brief moment we spent resting in the hotel room, we had been drinking and snorting nonstop. We were hitting all the clubs we knew. Rick was apparently having a good time but I was getting tired of it all.

I was starting to think that this 58-year-old Mohican-style motherfucker was never going to call it a day. During my time with Rick, I noticed how he was able to go long and hard. He would not mix his drinks; he would only drink Jack and Coke and he would balance it out by having measured sips of Jack Daniels and every two hours one line of Speed. I had to try and break that routine up. If

I could prevent him from carrying out his normal routine, perhaps he would be stoned enough to finally give up, or he would generally call it a day to prevent himself from metaphorically falling off the wagon. So, the night before, I told him that there were a lot of cops from the Cross that often drink in these premises after their shifts so he shouldn't have lines on the table anymore. Incredibly, this did the job I wanted. By 8am on Tuesday morning, Rick was starting to show some break in his armour. His speeches were beginning to slur, and when he walked it was like he was on a string. Even he was beginning to notice that he was losing the battle against alertness. After a while, one of the noms from Bringelly walked into the bar and gave Rick the keys to his bike. It turned out that Rick had called all the noms while I was probably in the toilet. He was able to get one of them to bring his bike into town for him. He had suddenly decided in his mind that he wanted to go for a ride.

I was overjoyed; I would finally be rid of him. Actually, someone as stoned as he was shouldn't be riding but I wouldn't dare mention that, it would appear to him like another invitation. And to be honest, I couldn't go one more day with Rick around me. I would simply go insane. As far as I was concerned, he could ride himself off a cliff; I just wanted to be rid of him so I can get some sleep.

It was unbelievable that Rick had been going at it hard now for five days. The fact that he could still stand up amazed me, let alone the fact that he was about to ride his bike. I had never met anyone as staunch as that guy. Fuck knows where he wanted to go, but it seemed like his mind was made up, and you couldn't argue with Rick if he set his mind on something. I had no intention of asking him anything about his trip anyway. When he was ready to leave, he took his last sip – he made sure he finished the drink before him, at least – then he took the keys to his bike. He sent the nom back home and told me that he would meet me back at my place after he did something. I wondered what he planned to do. However, I didn't like the fact that he said he would come to my place. I didn't want him around anymore. He had nothing good to offer me besides drinking and snorting. Life should be more than that.

It turned out that he was feeling a bit randy and sometimes during the two days we were together in the Cross I had seen a girl give him her phone number and address so that's where he went. He had gone to get laid. Well, he needed it; perhaps that was going to clear his head. I caught a cab home and started to unwind. Because Rick wasn't taking any speed to keep him going the last six hours, I was. I had made four packages of speed wrapped in paper so I could swallow them when needed without Rick noticing. One hour passed and I was starting to get heavy on my couch. That's when I heard Rick's Harley pulling into my driveway.

What the hell! I couldn't believe what I had just seen. It was horror! Rick had come back to haunt me again. I hadn't thought he would return so fast. I was starting to get a hang on myself and here he was again. I began to blame myself for coming to the rescue of those noms. If I had not interfered, I wouldn't be suffering this way. It turned out that I might be the one who would find a high cliff to jump off after all. I couldn't imagine that

I would be able to endure any more of Rick's presence around me. He had come when I was about to have the rest that I had been denied for the last couple of days. I was starting to doze off to the noise from the construction work happening next door where they were building a new house, and that sound from Rick's Harley had me up on my feet and fully awake in seconds. The Harley was capable of bringing a dead Lazarus to life.

I opened my door and Rick came in looking like he just got out of bed fresh and rejuvenated. I was in horrors. This man's reputation did not do him justice. He sat down on my lounge. I made him a drink and pulled out the bong. I had intentionally brought out the bong. I wanted to knock him out by every possible means so that I could have the rest I so desired. I thought the bong was the only thing he hadn't had yet and maybe this could put him to sleep. So, we had a few cones, a few more drinks and some more coke. I even got the nitrous oxide out, a little trick I learned from Simon. He would take a drink, have a cone and with the rest of the space left in his lungs he would breathe into the nitro, holding it and the smoke from the pot in his lungs as long as possible. I was being methodical and it seemed like Rick was following my steps; he was trying to do everything I was doing. It was obvious that this was a strange experience for Rick. Perhaps he had thought that he would come and we would snort some speed. Of course, I had speed with me but I intentionally kept it away from Rick. Speed would not make me get what I wanted to achieve. Rather than knocking out Rick, it would only invigorate him. I didn't want that. I desperately wanted to get him off of me. If he took enough pot, I had no doubt in my mind that he would go to sleep. I would only have my desired rest if Rick's light was off. He had been following me around like a guilty conscience; it was high time for me to get rid of him in whichever way I could. But I admit, smoking the bong was not as fun as snorting coke, or taking Jack as the case might be. Even I preferred speed to filling my lungs with smoke from pot, but I wouldn't dare do that. I wouldn't go back to the same thing that damn near turned me into a breathing zombie. What would do the trick was enough pot to put the lights of both of us out. Sleep Rick! Sleep! Dammit! I felt like strangling him to be rid of him once and for all. And with the way things seemed to be going is that I might just end up doing that if he kept on going. I would strangle the life out of him and get rid of the body. It wouldn't be so hard to do anyway. The only challenge I would face, however, was how to get rid of his bike. Besides, I couldn't tell how many people had seen him ride into my driveway. The last thing I needed was series of tricky questions from the bored Detectives in the local precinct. But that was just me fantasizing of that moment, Rick was my brother now, and I would protect him like every other family member.

The whole time we were doing this it seemed like Rick was getting annoyed. It turned out that the noise from the work happening next door was getting to him. I sincerely hoped that was the case. Maybe he would not be able to take it anymore and he would just leave. And considering what he had been putting in himself the last couple of days, such kind of noise was the last thing he needed. He was getting to his limits and didn't want to hear any loud noises while he was winding down. The noise should bother me too but I had gotten used to it. When your house is beside the rail track, the noise from a train is inevitable, and you must learn to get over it or you may go crazy. The noise from the construction site was pissing Rick off so much that he questioned why I had chosen this particular apartment to pitch my tent. I only shrugged my shoulders and took my drink – I didn't give him any explanation. After I poured him his last drink he stood up with his drink and went to the back veranda of my apartment which was one storey above the construction workers. Rick leaned over, resting his elbows on the wooden rail, and started a conversation with the workers. I couldn't tell if he was in his right frame of mind or it was the alcohol that was talking. He was asking them what they were using, the type of tools they had and the floor plans of the building. You see as I have explained, Rick wasn't the type of person you ignored. He was always polite and respectful, but you could get the impression from him that if you disrespected him, he would turn into an animal. It seemed like the workers noticed that impression from him so they chose to oblige him. Usually, they would have ignored him and continued their work, but they could see that everything about Rick spelled trouble. And by looking at his face alone it was easy to tell that he was under an influence, either alcohol or drug.

The conversation went on. At this point all the tools were down and Rick had all the workers looking up at him on my veranda answering his questions. It suddenly dawned on me that Rick had deliberately engaged these workers in a conversation just to keep them from working, and ultimately preventing the annoying noise he obviously couldn't bear. I scoffed in fascination. Perhaps the workers themselves knew that he didn't appreciate the noise coming from them and it seemed like they didn't want to upset him, so they obliged him in the long conversation, which, by extension, seemed like an interview. Here I was inside on the couch watching Rick, drink in hand having a conversation with the workers next door about construction work. As a matter of fact, it seemed like Rick knew about the job as much as the workers, if not more. He was asking them questions that were strange to a layman like me; he was using construction terms that some of the workers didn't even understand. I was highly impressed by his knowledge. It turned out that the man wasn't entirely a hopeless case after all. Then all of a sudden, one of the workers decided to use his nail gun while he answered Rick's question. I supposed it was his way of saying that they had work to do; they could only engage Rick for so long since many of them were working by the time. But this didn't discourage Rick he continued asking them questions, some of them were repeated. The workers were getting frustrated, but Rick was determined to make sure they never continued the work. Then he did something incredibly insane. That was Rick; there was nothing he wouldn't do to get his voice heard, there was no line he wouldn't cross – he would not be ignored. First, he took off his boots as he continued talking to the men. This didn't raise any eyebrow as the day was sunny and they must have thought he was feeling too much heat. Then he took of his socks, still it was only natural to do so. When he started to take off his T-shirt, the workers began to stare at one another. It seemed to them like

Rick was trying to do something interesting. While he was taking all these off, he never stopped engaging them in conversation. At some point, he was the one answering his own questions as the workers were staring at him in surprise; even the guy with the nail gun was stunned. If Rick had stopped there the worker might have concluded that he was probably bored; but Rick didn't stop there. When he started taking off his pants, all the workers were bunched together looking up at him in utter shock. They couldn't believe what they were seeing as Rick removed all his clothes. Now they were looking up at him with those stares reserved for people of unsoundness of minds. Rick stood there, completely naked, with a drink in his hand, and waiting for them to answer his last question. To say the workers were embarrassed was a gross understatement; they couldn't bear to see that this madman was having a conversation with them.

Well, they didn't answer his question. Instead, they all packed up their tools, got into their Utes and took off. It was a little price to pay for the preservation of their dignity. They would come the next day to continue the work they couldn't complete. Hopefully, they wouldn't meet Rick when they come tomorrow. I hoped so too. Even though he had successfully stopped the workers from polluting the neighbourhood with their noise I was also embarrassed. He had both come to my help and humiliated me at the same time. Rick walked back into my room from the veranda, put his glass down (empty of course) and told me he was going to have a nap. I was grateful for this; I couldn't have heard better news at that time. Finally, at least for a couple of hours, I would be rid of Rick. It was now obvious that he had performed that stunt with those construction workers because he wanted to sleep. He would not be able to sleep through that noise. It was a smart and stupid move, but he got the job done. I didn't say a word; I allowed him to have his privacy and I went into my room where I eventually fell asleep. For the first time in days, I had a long sleep; it was what I had needed for so long. It was healing. When I woke up, I was as new as a baby. All the pains I initially felt were gone. Even the sores I had on my body where Rick had hit me with the paintball gun were starting to fade. My head was clear. When I went to check on Rick, I realized that he had left. I breathed a sigh of relief and went back to bed. I slept for the next two days.

I woke up on Thursday, the weekend of the Taren Point boys finishing up their probation and getting their full colours, so we had to get a few preparations done for that event. It was a long-awaited event; not all the noms would become bon fide Rebels, just the ones that were patched over. A lot of members from other clubs were invited to the event. It was like getting released from the slammers after a long sentence. Although it was only six months, it seemed like decades. Having to clean up after members, forcing you to wait up in members; you basically don't have your own life; your privacy is limited. You have no choice but to slave away yourself for these six months. Of course, you are allowed to party and have drinks with the members, but you have to know your place – people like Rick were always available to stretch you out to the limit. But like I already mentioned, unlike the other noms, I knew my way around; I was already a

Rebel, it was only not yet official. I didn't do the heavy-lifting like the other noms who had to go through a whole lot. The day finally came. All the Taren Point boys were now Rebels and I had another big week of partying with life members. At one point we ended up back at Taren Point with two of the old members, Simon and Bear. We had been going hard for three days, with Simon and Bear wanting to remind these new blokes that they still had to watch how they portrayed their colours; it was just normal routine. It was a warning, to remind the new Rebels that they didn't have to be careless even though they were now promoted. I ended up trashing the Taren Point club house with Bear and Simon. The next day I had to hire the cleaner to clean it. Now that all the Taren Point boys were full members, me and the Turk were the only ones in that chapter who had to do the work, so I was hoping Bear would find the new premises for me and the Turk to serve out our last 6 months before our vote was called to get our full colours.

Mardi Gras

Two months after the Taren Point chapter got their colours, Bear still didn't have a site for the city chapter. He was busy setting up a tattoo shop in Cronulla, so he didn't have time. He was getting frustrated; he needed help badly. The Turk and I noticed his frustration and chose to help him find a place (Turk was the guy that hung around Bear for two years before nomming up at the same time as me). We did as we promised; we helped Bear find a site for the city chapter; he was very grateful for that. But before Bear, the Turk and I left Taren Point we had one more weekend there – a weekend of partying hard and meeting new and interesting people.

It was the weekend of the Sydney Gay and Lesbian Mardi Gras. I was summoned to Bringelly to pick up the "City" patch for our vest and I was in no rush to get back to Taren Point just to serve drinks to Chief and his boys, especially on Mardi Gras weekend. Having to pick up the patch was an escape for me, and I decided to take as much time as I could. But eventually I knew I had to go back because, a day before, Chief had organized a photographer artist friend of his to take a few shots of the Taren Point chapter, re-creating the last supper with our vests on. The photographer was an understanding guy so we were free to display whatever. We knew he would keep the photographs highly private – he wouldn't want his head on a spike if he acted carelessly. The fact that he was a friend of Chief didn't mean he would not be punished if he behaved stupidly. We ended up taking photos with a few different styles of poses, one with a few of us holding our guns up in the air or on the table. It was different. I like different; I enjoy having new pleasant experience. Of course, none of the photos with the guns were publicly released; only a few people had them, but the proper re-creation shots won a prize in Bondi a few months later.

I hung around Bringelly as long as I could but there was nothing happening there, so I jumped on my fat boy and headed back to Taren Point where I knew there was going to be life. That was me, I always looked out for fun. You would not find me in a boring environment. Life is short, and you only live once. You don't want to die knowing you didn't do what you wanted in life – you would be rolling over in your grave, disappointed in yourself. That is not me, I would not allow that on myself. That is why I party as hard as I can, I meet as many people as I can. I didn't put any restriction on myself. Whatever was fun, you should count me in.

And so, on my way to Taren Point, as I was going through the City, I was reminded that it was Mardi Gras by all the half-naked men and women covered in glitter. I also remembered hearing somewhere that Kylie Minogue was making a guest appearance at one of the parties being held at the Hordern Pavilion. It was at that very moment that I rode past the pavilion; as I rode past, I saw heaps of sexy women, or at least I thought they were women. They were looking sweet enough to be eaten with a spoon; some wonderful boobs packaged in some soft-looking bikini, and their ass cheeks that beckoned to me to come over. As much as I would have loved to have any of those sexy damsels, something else made me turn back. Something else took my attention, something more striking than the women. There was a bus parked near the entrance to the pavilion and on that bus were these big banners with the words "REPORT DISCRIMINATION HERE". That's when my mind came up with the idea of how I could kill a bit of time and amuse myself at the same time.

Permit me to set the scene for you here. I was a bloke in leather that didn't look like all the other guys in leather; I looked particularly different, but everyone could tell that I belonged in a bike club, considering the way I was attired. I was riding a bike and wearing a leather vest that had a motorcycle club (MC) patch on it and gold rings on every finger; if that didn't spell a kind of signal, I wonder what would. I knew I wasn't going to get in – they wouldn't allow someone of my sartorial delight an entry into such a party of people who considered themselves more respectable; and of course, my presence would give them an impression of impending trouble, and those folks, to a degree, appeared to be easy-going. They didn't want someone of my reputation in their party. Besides, my dressing was a bit of misnomer for that kind of gathering, and I knew it, but I wanted to give them a taste of their own medicine. I parked the fat boy right beside the entrance, took my skull cap off and walked to the back of the line. I knew I had no business being there; in fact, what they were doing there was of absolutely no interest to me but I wanted to have a good time just ruffling their feathers. Everyone was looking at me strangely; I knew that kind of look – I expected it, I basked in it. The more confused they were the better for me. They looked all around the outside of the venue to see if there were more like me here to crash their party. But I was there on my own with no intention or wrecking anyone's party. I was just amusing myself. I had no intention of bringing them any trouble, except of course if they brought the trouble to me, and, as always, I would reward them in double. I sincerely hoped none of them would try anything foolish. I had just come here to amuse myself. It would be a shame if I turned their lovely party bloody just because some of them decided to act stupid.

I knew what I needed to do. Like I said, I wanted to give them a taste of their own medicine. I located the pay booth and pulled out a bundle of 100s from my wallet. I could notice the confused expression on the face of the guy in the booth. I wanted to smile but managed to hide the grin forming on my face. As I approached the booth, the guy finally decided to pull the "only members line" on me. That was exactly what I was expecting.

"Really?" I said, feigning surprise and embarrassment. "What do you mean by only members only?"

The guy looked further confused and replied, I'm so sorry, sir. That's the rule. This line is for members only. You can find another booth a few blocks away from here."

The guy looked genuinely apologetic and polite. Most of other people would have just asked me to go and have a sexual intercourse with myself; and that would have resulted in violence, of course. This guy seemed to be scared of me. It appeared to him that I represented trouble and messing with me was the last thing he wanted to do. I admired his wisdom; he was a man who knew how to stay out of trouble. Who would want to hurt someone as polite as that young man? I liked him already, but I was just having fun.

"Okay, thank you for pointing that out," I said and walked straight to the bus to report my case of straight man discrimination, or discrimination against bikies; I wasn't sure which way to go yet. Then I walked up the two steps into the bus and sat down in front of in front of the first guy taking complaints.

"I have come here to lodge a complaint," I told the guy.

"About what, sir?" he asked without looking up from what he was writing.

"About discrimination."

This seemed to catch his attention for he looked up. His eyebrows were hoisted aloft as he stared at me. He was just noticing me for the first time. He looked surprised.

I sat there for five minutes explaining how this happened to me all the time because I was a bikie. I put up a convincing expression of hurt that would have impressed a movie director (that was the angle I decided to go with).

"I don't think it's fair that I should be treated this way," I added, "I am a human being like every other person. I expect to be treated with fairness and respect."

The young guy taking my complaint was a great listener. He did not flinch the whole time (that's after getting over the shock of my appearance); he didn't give a smirk either, no eye-rolling, no you-have-got-to-be-kidding-me – he was all business. I had never seen someone more professional. He calmly wrote down my complaints. I watched as he scribbled something illegible into his little book. When he was done, he stood up and asked me to come with him. As I followed him, I thought as long as it was not an underground bunker, he was taking me too, I was willing to see where he was taking me.

He walked straight to the front of the Hordern Pavilion and I followed him like a lamb. He pushed his way past the poor guy dressed as an angel paying his entrance fee and started ripping the guy in the pay booth a new one. It was hilarious but I hadn't anticipated it getting as far as it did. I felt a little bad for the courteous and polite young man that was being torn apart. I didn't think he should be treated that way; he was a very respectful chap who thought he was only doing his job. Whatever I did was not personal; I was just goofing around. I just wanted to have a story for the boys of how I was discriminated against by our LGBTI community, but this guy was going on with it; it didn't seem like he would be stopping anytime soon. He gave the guy in the booth a good cleaning of the earwax. His actions were soon attracting the attentions of everyone around and they were beginning to stare. I almost laughed out loud at the drama I had caused. After he finished with him, he pulled me in next to him, and the guy in the booth apologized to me and gave me a stamp to get in. As I collected the stamp, I winked at the guy and left. I had an intention of later returning to him and apologizing for what I made him go through. Truly, he didn't deserve to be treated that way. It would have been perfect had the man behind the booth been a rude fellow. Surely, I would have made him deficient of a few teeth before going ahead to report him. I would have caused a more serious drama than what had just happened – but I had encountered a polite man. Such kinds of people were rare to come by, especially in my kind of lifestyle. I wondered what the guy was doing in that booth. He would have gotten a job in a Fortune 500 company or something. That was the kind of place people like him should belong, not in the economical slum of the world.

Now I was the one in shock at how the whole situation eventually panned out. Actually, I didn't expect the man to lash out at the man in the booth as he did, let alone asking him to apologize to me and issuing me the stamp. I had thought the man would not give me audience when I went to report to him. I had thought he would judge me by my dressing and ask me to leave – I thought he would simply act like the man in the booth, but in a less polite manner. If that had been the case, I would have caused a lot more trouble than they wanted there. Even though I was just there to mess around I would not stand around and allow myself to be treated like a bum.

I thanked the guy in the booth and the gay rights worrier before making my way in. I had never expected to get this far so I thought I will stay close to the exit and have one or two drinks before heading back to the club house; whatever was going on here was strange to me, and I had no intention of attracting more attention to myself than I had already done. In reality, I was done with the fun. Whatever I had wanted to achieve had been achieved. I wasn't interested in joining their party or however they chose to hold their own party; but then again, I decided that it wouldn't hurt terribly if I tarried there a few moments longer just to watch how things were being done there. There I was inside the Hordern Pavilion, drink in hand, ass up against the wall near the exit and observing my surroundings. That's when I noticed a couple of burly men having a drink about 10 feet away from me and looking in my direction. All I could guess from the way they were staring at me was that they felt I didn't belong in that club, or, by some way, they saw my little drama with the man by the booth and the superior gentleman. I looked back in the men's direction. I didn't make any attempt to make any kind of contact with them, I just stood in my corner watching them. I didn't know what their impression about me was and so I couldn't give them the proper response based on what they thought of me. One guy was about 130kg wearing a leather vest, leather G-String and leather chaps, nothing else. He had a hairy chest and belly popping out of his vest and handlebar moustache with a bald head. The other guy was about 100kg, also wearing a leather vest with a pair of leather pants, love hearts cut out of where the back pockets should have been. He also had a big moustache and beard. Judging by their appearance, I suspected that they were the gay community version of bikies, and here I was in their territory, I was starting to get nervous, I have never been in a situation like this and I didn't know how to react, all I knew was to keep my ass up against the wall and make no one slips something in my drink.

So, there I was facing these two bear-like men wearing leather, looking at me. Then they suddenly smiled and I relaxed my nerve. I had originally tensed myself for an attack. I was already fully aware of my surrounding. I stood close to where I could easily reach for a couple of bottles I could use for a weapon. I knew the guys were a lot bigger and probably more powerful than me. I might be able to take one but I couldn't beat both of them in a fair fight – well, there was nothing fair about two men against one man. So, the only way I could defend myself against these two bears was if I used the bottles to my advantage. All I would need to do was nick a few arteries off their bodies and they would be as useless as a pair of condoms. But thankfully, I wouldn't have to do anything violent tonight. Their smile was an indication that they had friendly intentions towards me.

All of a sudden, I looked towards the stage because something was happening and I thought it might be Kylie, but it was only the MC announcing a DJ. When I looked back towards the two guys sussing me out, I noticed their group had grown by three – another equally large man had joined them. I exhaled with a feeling of both relief and surprise. From all indication, it didn't appear that the man just joined them. He seemed to have been with them from the start. He probably left to take a leak or something. Now if a fight had broken out between me and the men, I would be fighting two men without knowing that there was a third guy around. The most dangerous kind of fight was the one where you don't know who your enemy is; you will simply be fighting blindly, and that's an advantage for your opponent who knows about your ignorance. There was no way I would be able to win any fight with those men as long as there was a third party someone. He could simply appear from nowhere and just knife or hit me on the head with something heavy and shut my lights out. But here is a shocker; if I had thought the men were three, I was gravely wrong. They were five! Five hairy men! Even if I should fight them knowing their number, I would only be fighting for an escape; there was no way I would fight to beat all the five. Come on, I'm not Rambo for fuck's sake. I would simply fight my way to safety and get the hell far away from there as soon as possible.

Now there were five big hairy men covered in leather checking me out, smiling and lifting their drinks towards me as a sign of approval. I believe they expected me to come over and join them but for some reasons I refrained from doing such. Something didn't seem to jell right in me. I didn't know where the feeling had come from but I felt it was not proper for me to join them. Besides, I had no plan to be there for a long time. If I joined them now, I might be drinking with them all through the night, which, of course, was not my intention at all. However, I can't deny the fact that the men were friendly towards me, and it would be considered rude if I eschewed their friendly disposition towards me. Those were the kinds of things that often-caused brawls in the pub. The last thing I wanted was to anger these men; I think I already made my situation pretty clear. I didn't realize that in that dark environment they wouldn't be able to see my patch and know I was a real bikie. Seeing my patch could have caused one of two things; it could have broadened their smiles or it could have turned the smile to frowns, depending on what they thought about bikies, and ultimately what they would think about me. Well, because they couldn't see my badge, they just thought I was one of them and they were looking to recruit me into their little club. I was in over my head. All I could think of doing was to scull my drink and make my exit before they approached me. The last thing I would want was to be in the club of those men. That kind of lifestyle wasn't befitting for a person like me. But what's actually worse is that I might not be able to say no if they tried to recruit me; and if I remained there any longer, that might actually happen. I knew instinctively that this was the time for me to disappear from the scene. All the smiles and the raising of drinks to each other should end; I wasn't interested in joining their club, whatever it was. Don't get me wrong; I have nothing against the LGBTI community. What grown consenting people do is their business. I just didn't want to get caught in the middle; even though I have ultimate respect for their choice of sexuality, it's not something I look forward to practicing. Besides, I was a hardcore chap; I loved boobs and pussies too much to consider other forms of sexuality, or lifestyle as the case might be. So, I took off as soon as the opportunity presented itself; I jumped on my bike and rode straight to Taren Point a fast as possible. I had had enough; I wasn't going to stop for anything else, not even for any sexy girl. I just wanted to get to my safe spot. I arrived at the Taren Point club house. I said hello to everyone and jumped behind the bar never to mention that story to anyone. Of course, the irony of the situation was not lost on me.

That weekend passed and Turk, with me, started doing all the work on the new club house in the City. We had the opening night for the city chapter. It was a small club house so we kept it as a small event. We would only open our doors when needed.

3

CITY CHAPTER

Bear had already picked all the guys that would make up the City's chapter of the Rebels, and that was when I got to know Harry. Harry was a 10-year member and a very talented tattooist. Bear brought him in to work in his Cronulla tattoo shop, and so he was the man to go to whenever tattooing was required; he was responsible for a lot of drawings on the bodies of the Rebels. Everyone had said that he was the finest tattooist they ever knew. He drew with precision and perfection. In his profession he met a lot of cool and powerful guys among the Rebels; and because he was a cool guy himself, he was liked by most. Even I liked Harry straight away the moment I met him; he was a stand-up guy who treated everyone with respect. It was hard seeing Harry in a heated argument with anyone. He respected himself a lot, and the respect he accorded to people was always returned to him. He was like a lot of the members I had met in the last 8 months; he had lived a life that was jam packed. He was only six years older than me and he had already spent 10 years in the club, which is not an easy thing to do if you had experienced the lifestyle. Before joining the club, he was a soldier in the Australian Army. It was incredible that an ex-soldier of his status was that humble. When he got out of the ADF he took up boxing and that's when he joined up.

Like I already mentioned, Harry was also a very talented artist. Tattooing would be how he made his living, and he was devoted to it. He became the best in his business; he had chosen to make an honest living it was paying his bills for him. He was satisfied with his profession. He didn't have to do anything immoral or shameful to make money; he had a great reputation to protect even though he was a Rebel. Contrary to popular belief, not all bikies made a living from crime and Harry was a perfect example: no criminal record, always had a woman at home and made an honest living from his craft. He had no interest in drugs and violence. But that doesn't mean that Harry was a coward; if violence was unavoidable Harry could well protect himself. He was fit and skilled in boxing. I have heard some news about his violent days. There was one where he put three guys in the hospital when they were trying to harass his girlfriend. He and his girl had come out of a club in the night and were approaching their car when these three blokes suddenly appeared from nowhere. Apparently, they had been watching Harry and his woman in the club. They had seen the wad of cash in his wallet and were also eyeing the gold necklace the lady wore. The three men had accosted Harry with their knives and demanded he relinquished the wallet. Harry had obeyed them and given them the wallet without putting up a fight. But the men were greedy, they wanted the lady's necklace. Harry knew how important the necklace was for the girl so he had begged the men to forget about the jewellery. They already had his wallet that contained a lot of money; they didn't need the necklace. But the men had considered Harry's action confrontational. They had gone for him immediately. The first person to approach got kicked on the side of the neck and he went down like a house of cards. The second had tried to stab Harry but the ex-soldier twisted his arm at an acute angle and caused him to stab himself in the thigh. Then Harry had vented on the lone third man. He had beaten the man so badly that both eyes were swollen shut and his lips were split open. It was about half an hour after Harry and his woman had left that the men were discovered by one partygoer. Before leaving, Harry had taken his wallet. He would have left it but he didn't want any policeman questioning him. He had a clean record and he still wanted to maintain that clean sheet. Having a policeman question him, might not bode well for him. Besides, with the identity in his wallet, the men he had beaten might decide to press charges against him, even though they were technically the culprit. I think that was the last fight Harry ever had since that moment; he was never seen raising his voice at anyone or being rudely treated. Occasionally some drunks would try to frustrate him but others always came to Harry's rescue; he never had to do anything to defend himself, there were people who always had his back. Most people who didn't know Harry's history always thought him a peaceful man, and that never bothered Harry a bit. He didn't care about what anybody thought about him, it was what he thought about himself that mattered to him, and what his woman thought of him. That was the most important person in his life; I believe the woman was the person who made Harry the kind of person he was today. She was his life; if anything happened to her, the beast in Harry would be unleashed; and nobody would be prepared for that beast, not even me. So, because of Harry's reputation as a calm-headed person, he was one of the members that would make up the city chapter. There would be another seven members, just as interesting as each other but completely different.

The club house was finished and so were my party funds; I was dead broke now. I didn't realise how much I had been spending until this moment. Over the last 8 months I had spent like there was no tomorrow and I wasn't making any money, which was not supposed to be. I had been too careless. I had made such a lot of money that I hadn't thought that it would run out so soon. If I had known, I would have restricted my expenses. I wouldn't have been throwing money around in clubs like a drunken sailor. Now the money had finished and I was at the end of my wits. So, I started up again; I needed to bounce back to my feet; and to do that I would have to make a lot of compromise. First, I moved into an apartment in Glebe close to the club house and started doing my thing – the stuff that always brought me the money I needed. I had my eye on a few new toys and now that I was in my own chapter with Bear in charge. I had the time and the freedom I needed to make some money.

I didn't do much security work where I would have to carry a gun, but I did start selling coke again. That was one of the most profitable business I knew. Coke sells fast and it brings in fast money. A person in the coke business never runs out of money to spend. But pushing drugs is as dangerous as it is profitable. The moment you are caught by the cops then you are done for. The law frowns deeply on drug business, and the government has been on the battle against drugs for years, even before I was into the business – hell, even before I was born. But I had always been careful; so far so good, I had never been caught, and I intended to keep it that way. But at the back of my mind, I knew I was playing with fire. If I didn't stop, sooner or later I would be caught. Smart people who have been confident that they would never be caught are now rotting away in Federal Penitentiaries. My whole life I have always done well from coke; it was my major source of wealth. I can't think of any other business I could do that would rake in as much money as coke. Even security was not even close to the money realized from selling coke. Cocaine (coke) is the grandfather of all drug business. Once I had thought about opening a bar. I had realized that what people spend money more on after coke was booze. A lot of money could be realized from selling drinks, but I didn't think I would have the patience for that kind of lifestyle. I couldn't imagine myself standing behind a counter and serving drinks to people – that would be a dick move on my part. Besides, knowing how much I could drink myself, opening a bar would not be good for business, since I had the tendency of drinking more than I sold. With that, I would always run at a loss.

But it was different with coke; even though I took coke well, I couldn't take it every time. It must be regulated; if I took it as much as I took alcohol I would die of overdose. So, it was better to be in the coke business than in the booze. Honestly, selling coke seemed to be the only thing I knew I was really good at.

Since leaving school I would be introduced to many famous musicians through a school friend that went on to work for the EMI studios in the City as a sound engineer. So, every time he was doing a recording with a well-known artist and he couldn't get a hold of his usual coke supplier, he would call me. I was always his supplier; he chose me because I could make my delivery as discreet as he wanted. I always had five or six grams ready to go. I never did big amounts because I never had that addiction to money like so many people I would meet over the years, but I always made a considerable large sum of money from it – I just never allowed the zeal to get over my head. I just wanted to make enough to do what I wanted and that was to have a good time. So, I started selling again and at the same time I would fly over to different chapters all around the country just to meet these men. I had decided to meet my brothers and also make some new connections for my different endeavours. Knowing the kind of risk the business entailed, I only sold drugs when I had to. I guess that's what had been keeping my attention away from the police. Had I been a regular dealer I would most likely be in their wanted list by now. And, of course, if that were the case, arrest would be inevitable. The only thing I could do to prevent myself from being arrested was to totally disappear from the country. And I couldn't possibly do that anyway. Where would I go? I didn't know where I could go that would give me the kind of lifestyle I was used to here. No matter where I went, I would never feel at home. It would be hard leaving all the friends I had made over the years. Even with everything, I wasn't dumb; I didn't think I would sell coke for the rest of my life. I have always wanted to start a legit business that would bring in money constantly and I wouldn't have to always look out for the law. I wanted a business that would rake in so much money as from drug and it would still be legit. Well, I must be a wishful thinker.

The money started rolling in again and I started to spend big; I was back to my status. There is a kind of spirit about money. When you don't have it, you'll swear you will spend it wisely the next time you have I; but as soon as the money reaches your hand, sense flies out the window. I was spending as extravagantly as before, just the way it made the last money run out so fast. I couldn't help it. First, I bought a couple of sports cars – no singular, plural, cars. I was spending like someone without any plan for the rainy days. Well, I actually had no plan for any season. If the money ran out again, I would simply go back to my coke business and get the money back. The assurance that I would always get the money back made me spend as carelessly as I could. I was buying things I didn't need simply to keep up appearance. After buying the cars, I took over the payments for a 40-foot Sea Dancer. My time by the water in the party house I was living in before the Glebe apartment had given me a new love for the water; now I craved it. I have loved the water all my life, but I had forgotten what it was like for a long

time. So, when I was living along the bay, I bought a few
watercrafts, but nothing like the Sea Dancer. It looked like
one of those Miami Vice speed boats but under the deck it
was all luxury: double bed in the front cabin with a port
hole that opened up to the front deck, lounge area and
kitchen, shower and toilet and finally, at the back under
the rear deck, another double bed. It was powered by
two V8 engines. It was great. It cost a fortune, but it was
worth the money. It was my personal small paradise on
water. I had a great time having a party in it. Sometimes
I would spend days just in it. I had an abundant supply
of alcohol and friends visited; so, every day was a feast. I
went to bed with a different girl every night. I was living
my life to the fullest. My status in the club was elevated.
I was more respected than before. I was rich, bold and
well-connected. Everyone who knew me was adequately
taken care of. Every weekend, we would have a large party
where strippers would come in to entertain the guests. It
was always wild right there in the Sea Dancer. The music,
the drinks, the drugs, the sex – hell, there was orgy and
all kinds of kinky stuff.

I took out five strippers on the day I made the deal
with the previous owner. We first went into Darling
Harbour. I was at the controls talking to the previous
owner and the girls were spread out, three on the front
deck topless with just G-strings on and the other 2 girls
on the rear deck also in their swimmers but topless. I
remember all the tourists taking photos of us. After that
the girls wanted to go somewhere to swim. I took them to
the back of Taronga Zoo; I don't know why but it seemed
like a good place at the time. So, I dropped anchor and

the girls jumped off. After a while I was feeling mischief again; I wanted to recreate what I did with the community so I told the girls, "You know that there's sharks in there."

I never seen anything like that before; one minute they were all just swimming and floating around the back of the boat and the next minute they were swimming over each other trying to get back in. It was incredibly funny to watch them as they scampered for safety in my boat. They were screaming and swimming as fast as they could. I had a good time watching as their boobs and asses bounce as they swam frantically. I guessed most of the girls had watched the movie *Jaws* and did not want to be a victim of a rogue shark that would take bites off their limbs. I felt a bit bad for doing it, but it was still funny for a few seconds.

When they had climbed up to the boat, I smiled at them and told them I was only kidding. But I actually wasn't kidding; there were sharks in the water; they were everywhere in the harbor, but their attack was very rare. The girls were pissed at me for my prank, but they didn't attempt to jump back into the water. I had created enough fear in them to go back to that fun. So, we spent most of the time in the boat partying away. They were my first guests in the boat, those girls knew how to party hard; they gave me the fun of my life. We rode in the boat all across the water and the girls enjoyed every moment of it. A lot of them went topless as we sped on water; their boobs were firm and perky, and I could see some men from the other boats ogling at them as we passed by them. They were actually begging the girls to leave my boat and join them. I found it incredibly amusing. I wouldn't have faulted any of the girls if they had decided to join those men. They were strippers anyway. But they didn't; they chose to be with me.

Still, after that little scare the girls would not go back in the water no matter how much I tried to persuade them. So, I dived in. Again, the idea to fool around occurred to me. I was having as much fun as I could. I enjoyed how I was teasing the girls and the previous owner of the boat. In my left hand I was holding an oxygen cylinder about the size of a 500ml bottle of water. It was for emergency air when you're scuba diving. It had its own mouthpiece and regulator on it and you could stay under water for about five minutes. I dived into the water keeping the oxygen out of sight as the girls were watching me from the back of the boat. I was telling them how safe it was, and that there's nothing to worry about. I was only showing them that it was safe to swim in the water. Even knowing that the water teemed with shark, I wasn't afraid. There had never been any case of shark attack in a long time. It would not be now that the sharks would choose to attack. I was swimming in the water and the girls were watching me. Some of them were even pleading that I should get out of the water, that it wasn't as safe as I thought it was. I continued swimming round and round. Then I suddenly stopped; it was time for me to pull my prank. That's when I started to yell and splash around. I was crying for help and getting myself submerged as if something was pulling me into the water. The girls and the man were all agitated. They were running around the deck and screaming like chickens with their heads cut off. I found the scene so funny to watch. As soon as I got close to the rear deck I dived under the boat and put the mouthpiece in so I could breathe. I sat there for three minutes and not one person jumped in, not even the previous owner. I understood the philosophy of life at that moment. There are some people in life that no matter how much you take care of them, no matter how much you showed you care about them, they would never risk their own safety to protect or rescue you. I surfaced at the front of the boat and I could hear all the screaming. That was all they could do, that was everything they would do – they would scream just to show they cared. No, they would not do what was necessary; their scream was the only help they could render. It was hilarious to imagine. As soon as they saw me with the oxygen bottle in my mouth, everything within reach on the boat was thrown at me. Some of them actually took offence and said what I did was not funny. They pretended to care so much about me and I found the pretence somewhat cute. I was apologizing to them even when I knew that I wasn't supposed to, but I was having a good time. It meant nothing to say I was sorry; I didn't mean it anyway. Besides, there was nothing good alcohol and coke would not fix. After that I took them to a more secluded spot and made up for my antics with plenty of booze and drugs. They had the best time of their lives. The girls didn't want the fun to end.

Weeks went by. I was breaking every rule I had set for myself over the years that kept me off the law's radar. Being discreet was what had kept me off the attention of the cops for so long, but I was in a bike club now and I hadn't realized that with my membership came extra interest in what I was doing. During this time, I even started doing a few jobs for the Fixer. The Fixer was an old friend of mine. He grew up and went to school in Dulwich Hill like me. He was sent to prison for a short time for drugs and that is what made him change the way he did things. Instead of even getting his hands dirty again by dealing and handling drugs again, he chose a more suitable position for his type of personality and skills, that's how he become known as the Fixer. He got to know everyone and anyone worth knowing in the Sydney and Melbourne underworld, while maintaining a persona of a legitimate businessman, he did this by opening up a number of different businesses such as restaurants and other renown businesses where it didn't look out of place for a well-known underworld figure would frequent, this is where the Fixer would do most of his business. He could sit down with his guests and organize whatever needed organized without the authority's taking any notice of him. So, this is how the Fixer made his money, he would introduce people with certain skills to other people who needed their services and if the connections made money for both parties then the Fixer would get a percentage of that enterprise. For example, let's say there was one drug dealer making a lot of money in his area and another drug dealer moves into his area and also starts selling in the same area, the profit margin is split in two, so this is where the Fixer comes in, the first dealer would tell the Fixer his predicament and the Fixer would introduce him to someone like me. I would go and shut down the second dealer and whatever I took from him was mine, so if I got $100,000 in cash or drugs, I would give the Fixer 20% for the job and the first dealer would also pay him something for restoring his profit margin, that's how the Fixer made his money, and he needed a lot of it, even though he might have looked a legitimate businessman. He lived his life like us, he would spend thousands on hookers every week and thousands more on the horses, so the money coming in from his legitimate businesses was not enough. Out of all of us making our money on the streets the Fixer was the most secured. It would be very hard for the cops to connect him to anything illegitimate because he was always extremely careful in his dealings. The only thing he could be charged for would be using hookers which was not really a crime the last time I checked. The Fixer also liked to smoke a joint at the end of every day but again that's not something that would send him back to jail. It was through the Fixer I got to meet and party with one of Melbourne's smartest and most successful underworld figures. At first, the Fixer told me a friend of his was coming to Sydney to bet on the horses and he, the Fixer, wanted me to tag along because this guy would have a lot of money with him. So, I understood he wanted someone with a gun with him to make sure he and his group weren't robbed but what I didn't know was how much money this guy would be bringing with him every time he came down. Even without knowing the amount of money, I chose to take the job. It was a favour to the Fixer; he had helped me out in the past with many good jobs and I could tell this one would also pay off. I had a lot of stuff going on for myself and I could have easily refused this request, but the Fixer was a personal friend; I always managed to look after this guy for him and I did, that is how I got involved with the Gambler.

The Fixer and the Gambler

The Gambler was a Melbourne underworld figure that was introduced to me by the Fixer in the early 90s.

He would often come to Sydney with about $1 million just to bet on the horses. I would be invited by the Fixer because of my knowledge about security and my calmness. You see many bodyguards working for underworld figures were basically just thugs, good with their fists but not known for their thinking and negotiations skills. I on the other hand, hated physical violence and only used it as a last resort. I have always had the ability to de-escalate a situation that would have otherwise ended up in a physical alteration. Plus, the Gambler always had his thugs around him anyway since the event of the drive-by attack; I was only there for peace of mind, so they knew there was at least one person with them who had a gun and knew how to use it. The Gambler must have been very important to the Fixer to have recommended me to him; he could have easily gotten one of the thugs and send him to the Gambler but he wanted me. And I could guess that the Gambler had paid him a cool sum of money to help him find a professional – so he called unto me to take up that position. My job was not actually much with all the Gambler's thugs around. I was always there only to observe things and take decision actions for the Gambler before things went awry. I was usually quiet and just observe the surroundings.

So, one weekend the Gambler invited me and the Fixer to Melbourne just to show his appreciation. That's the kind of guy he was; he would look after everyone associated with him. Unlike many others in his line of work, the Gambler shared his wealth with everyone around him. The Fixer and I flew to Melbourne. I didn't need a gun this time so we flew there. The Gambler put us up in a $3,500 a night room in one of Melbourne's most extravagant hotel and he hired three hookers to stay with us 24 hours a day for the two days we were there. It was like being in paradise; I thought I had been living an extravagant lifestyle but this experience showed me how wrong I had actually been. The hotel suites were like the gates of heaven. Everything I wanted were provided; and the women were the most delicious pieces of ass I'd ever seen. I wanted the experience to last forever. The Gambler was obviously incredibly rich to have lodged us in a place like this. No wonder he needed a bodyguard that would ensure that he was never robbed, and he could afford to hire those thugs that followed him around everywhere. Even the Fixer was impressed by the hospitality we enjoyed in the hotel.

He also left one of his boys with us just in case we needed something that you couldn't buy from the corner store. I worked out later he was also there in the capacity I would have been if we were in Sydney; he wasn't just a regular thug, he was a calculative and highly experienced bodyguard. He was younger than me but there was no denying the fact that he knew his beans. I didn't even want to imagine who would win if both of us locked horns. In a way, he seemed to have a slight advantage over me; he was younger and probably more agile. He was a trained fighter whereas I learnt my own fighting skills in the streets. There was a big possibility that he might beat me senseless in a physical combat; but then again, I might be more experienced than him, which would be the only advantage I might have over him. If I ever beat him it would be because of the experience I had. This young kid was known as Benji. He was an up-and-coming kickboxer and a very pleasant young man; he was also quite professional in his dealings; unlike the other thugs that watched over the Gambler. Benji never gave an air of superiority over us, or anyone else for that matter. He was just pleasant and only doing the job he was required to do. He was also a good observer, just like me. I liked him already. He escorted us everywhere to the restaurants and clubs, and then back to our hotel room. The Gambler had taken us to all the exclusive nightclubs. This was a different style of partying for me but not unfamiliar.

We partied hard that weekend and the Fixer took full advantage of the hookers. For me, knowing that they were being paid to look after us didn't really do it for me. Don't get me wrong, I had a laugh with the girls. But if I don't know whether the girls are into me for me, or are just going it for money, it just doesn't turn me on. I suppose all my years in the Cross dealing with girls in the industry sort of turned me off, knowing how some of them felt dealing with customers. So even if they seem to be right into it, I can't be sure. So, when there's money involved, I prefer not to be. So, while the Fixer had a nice time with them, I just kept my relationship with the girls simply platonic. That's me – sometimes I could be wild and other times I could be morose. This time around, I chose to not get rally involved with those girls even though they were very exotic and appealing. I just didn't want to be one of their 'clients' that would soon be forgotten in their minds. I always preferred those girls that would engage me in interesting conversation and genuinely show that they were into me even though they were hookers. I guess that's a skill that should also come with 'hooking'; they should be able to make clients feel like they were the best thing that had happened to them, it's all about being very good at anything one does; the deception should be a part of the perks that should come with the job. It's just too easy to meet a hooker and just get her to bed; there's no excitement, no chase, no convincing – these were the elements that would make the eventual sex actually worthwhile. Perhaps this was why hookers like Kitty and Angie were successful in their businesses. They were able to get men to do things for them; they brought something new to the table, something challenging, girls like this could make you feel so special that you start to believe that they feel for you. I can only respect women like that, it can't be easy doing what they do, but I suppose if you are motivated in achieving something, then you can also do anything you put your mind to. But back to Glebe, so there I was breaking every rule I had set for myself.

Glebe

I was having so much fun now that I slowly began to slip off. I was beginning to do things I would never do in some normal situations. I was snorting plenty of coke, driving around in flashy cars and partying hard nearly every night. I didn't know that purchasing those exotic cars would garner more attention than I had anticipated. I was doing everything in excess. The loud party every night was bound to pique someone's interest. And if there was a neighbour whose loud music had been affecting, surely such a neighbour would call the police to report the situation. On many occasions the police had knocked on my door during party and had asked that the volume of the music be reduced because the neighbours were complaining. I had not seen anything wrong about that since the police never attempted to break into the party and search for hard drugs.

Usually when I did business I would not party at the house or apartment I was living in at the time, but not this time. Every day and night there were people at the apartment; it was always filled with guests. There were times when a lot of them would sleep over. Some who couldn't keep up would just crash out there. There was no real food in the house; what anyone could have in excess was the drugs and the booze. I guess that was what had been attracting a lot of people into my apartment; many of them I couldn't even recognize. I was sure there were a few I had never seen before in my life. And I didn't care; they had all come to have fun and I was in a good position to give it to them – my door was always open for everybody, both male and female – well, the female had to be beautiful and extremely sexy. I was living life at full throttle and heading straight for a brick wall. I would party every night with club members and associates, and in the mornings, I would call all the legitimate business owners I was doing business with and try to deal with whatever projects I had with them. In-between all that, I would catch two to three hours sleep here and there; it was just an off and on thing. Sometimes when I was sleeping, a sudden noise from the sound system would wake me, or a member might need my attention. I never got more than occasional two or three hours of shuteye.

I also had a hooker friend of mine come in three times a week to service my apartment and me; whenever she came, she was exclusive for my service. The others could take any of the available girls in the house but this particular hooker was mine whenever she came. In fact, it wasn't only anytime I was having a party that she would come. Sometimes she would make an appearance when the party was over. She would finish her shift at one of Sydney's top brothels and come straight to my place. She had her own keys so if I was out or sleeping, she just let herself in. She would clean my place up naked and if I wasn't there she would just crash in my bed until I got back. I always loved coming home to meet her waiting for me on the bed, naked under the sheet and inviting me over for a meal of her gorgeous body. If I was there it was very rarely, she got through all the housework before I had her bent over some piece of furniture or spread out on my bed. It was always hard for me to watch her clean naked without having to drag her away and enter her. She was available for everything I wanted. I would screw her at every angle, every position I could think of. And she was a great lover too. Whichever way I wanted her to react she was available. If I wanted her to be passive, she would give her body to me and put herself at my mercy. This was often the case; but on some occasion I would be too tired to do the heavy lifting. So, I would just lay there and let her work on me. She was very professional; she gave the best head any man could ever want. Whenever she worked on my crotch, my toes were always at the receiving end as they would curl and I would be sent to cloud nine. The things she could do with her tongue and her teeth, then those hands stroking my shaft as she sucked me – I'm telling you; she was the best, and I always looked after her well and she always come with her A-game. This is how things were until I got my colours.

So, it was a Thursday night and the members from the city chapter were summoned to Bringelly for the monthly meeting where all the chapters in Sydney would meet once a month to discuss any issues or upcoming events. This was also the night they were going to vote on whether I get my colours or whether I had to do another 3 months as a nom, but I knew I would get the vote to become a full member and I was ready for it. The vote was cast and it was unanimous. I was now a full member of the Rebels motorcycle club. The way these things go is that once you get your colours you must pay for all the drinks that night, and I did, all that night, the next and the one after that. It started at Bringelly but didn't end there. After everyone had enough there, Bear, Simon and Brownie wet back to the city club house, Brownie was the national Vice President, an absolute Gentleman. Brownie grew up in the country and he was a very talented boxer before the Bargwa took him under his wing. Brownie could mix with business leaders, officers of the law, outlaws, family people or just your local homeless person outside the club, and one thing you could be sure of he would treat them all equally and with the same respect. Then you have Simon; well, what can I say about Simon? He was just a machine. Everything he did was at a different level, whether it was racing bikes or fighting. He had a fearlessness about him that I could not explain; I thought I was a daredevil, but I wasn't close to the kind of daring heart of Simon. It's one thing to have the guts to do something, but to have the guts and the idea in your head that failure is not an option? That's Simon. Finally, there's Bear, the person that showed me there were others out there like me and brought me into my new family. I respect these three guys a lot; I didn't think there was anything I would not do for them. If I was in a pickle and I needed people to come to my aid, these three people were my shield. With them around there was nothing we would not be able to achieve. There was Brownie who could negotiate with anyone. There was no one in this world that Brownie could not approach and have a perfect dialogue with. He could have a good chat with the President of the United States. Simon was there for when things went sour. If it was violence Simon was a master of that. He was a great fighter who could handle anybody. When I say anybody, I mean anybody. I had once seen him fight, and boy, was that a bloody fight. He was fast, athletic, and skilled. And Bear was a master planner. As far as I know, Bear has no violent bone in his body. He knew how to get himself out of trouble. He was good at providing solution to things without having to resort to violence. He was a master negotiator. He could talk a snake out of its skin. Bear had such a personality that no one would want to hurt him. Instead of hurting him, they would give him whatever he wanted.

So finally, after a full week of partying, everyone had gone home and I was back at it, making money. Yeah, I would need to get back what I had expended. I had the son of a prominent Adelaide politician come over to pick up his weekly package of coke, then I had two members from the Adelaide chapter stay at my place for a few days while they got rid of all the hydro, they brought down from Adelaide so they could buy some coke and speed to take back. When they left that night, I had a girl come over after she finished her shift at Dancers. It was now a regular routine; having a girl over at my place, especially after partying so hard. In a way, being with a girl seemed like the perfect method of getting rid of all the junk I had put inside myself during the partying. The sex was a form of exercise to me; an exercise I knew I needed. It had helped me a lot to stay nimble and agile. I believe that without the sex, all the alcohol and drugs would have done some great damage to me, for I knew I was having them in excess, and I had no time for any doctor's appointment. I believed only pussies keep appointment with doctors. The only way I would ever need a doctor was if I were shot and needed to get the bullet out, or I was stabbed to the point of death. Besides surgery, every other thing could go to hell as far as I was concerned. And luckily for me, I never really had any health issue; I was always the best version of myself. The last time I actually was in a doctor's office was when I was a teenage and suffered a severe case of stomach ache, and of course, even then the ache was so much that I had to be operated on.

Of course, I had had various wounds from violence, but I had not had any reason to make use of a doctor. Whenever something like that happened my folks were always available to nurse me back to my feet. If anyone were shot and they needed to get the bullet out, all they would use was a pair of pliers and alcohol. I know it sounds crude but that was just how it was. We all knew that going to the hospital was never a good idea. There was always the possibility of the doctors calling the police. We always tried to stay away from the cops as much as possible. Their presence had never been of benign companionship. They were always going about making their little investigations and uncovering things they didn't need to know about. So, it was a code on the streets that hospital should be the last, last resort if anything happened to any one of us. Whatever happened, we should be able to solve it on our own.

Raid

I had seen this girl a few times and she seemed different from what I was used to; she was particularly unique on her own. I had met a lot of girls over the years and I can tell you that I have had the best of the best. But this particular girl seemed like a unique brew; something that had never been tasted. No, I'm not talking about virginity; I'm talking about her grace, her poise, the way she spoke, the way she carried herself, her diction. She was from a different world; she could as well have been an alien from a strange planet. Relating with her was a new experience; I thought I had had every experience imaginable; I couldn't believe that this particular one was taking me to another new state, an unfamiliar level. I didn't know what it was at that point, but my gut told me to see where this went. I wasn't looking for a relationship because I was dealing, but my gut has never led me astray.

I saw Jane that morning. Later she left because she had her young daughter, Reese, at her sister's house where she lived. Jane always made sure she was home before her daughter woke up so she could get her ready for school. Every morning she would wake up and made food for her child. Then Jane would walk her to school, go back home to sleep, get up and walk her back home and spend the rest of the day with her until it was time for bed. Late in the night when her daughter had slept off, Jane would go to Dancers and strip all night, only to do the same thing again the next day. I suppose that was one thing about Jane I respected so much. Another thing was she had no interest in taking drugs. Don't get me wrong, she could party just as hard as any member in my club, but she could handle it and never went out of her way to get drunk. She was a class of her own; and even though she had a growing daughter Jane had one of the most beautiful bodies I had ever beholden. She was incredibly beautiful, even more striking in appearance than a lot of the other strippers in Dancers. Most of the men around always wanted to be with Jane because of the way she related with people around her. She had never gone wrong in the eyes of anyone. She knew her job and she did it well. I could even notice that a lot of the other girls were envious of her. Some of them wanted to act like her but they just couldn't; they weren't wired like she was. While the girls would drink and snort to stupor, Jane always knew when to call it quits. No one had ever seen Jane drunk; none had succeeded in getting her drunk either.

The cab came to get Jane. When Jane left, a Nomads friend of mine popped in to get some coke. After he left, I was on the phone talking to my mechanic. He had a friend of mine at his workshop helping him set up the alarm system for a car I was building. This guy was one of the best car thieves in Sydney and he was setting up a system that was thief proof. Ironic, right? A car thief setting up an alarm system that would prevent thieves from stealing a car. Well, he knew about all the tricks any thief could employ to steal a car and he was working his alarm against all those kinds of tricks. If he were successful, the car I was building would be one of the most secure cars. It's just like the old trick of keeping your money safe in the hand of someone who might want to steal it. By keeping your money with a thief, you have secured that money. Of course, he would not want to steal money that he had been tasked to keep secure. If anything happened to that money, he knew he would be responsible for it. It was an old system in the book. It was that logic that made me employ a professional car thief to help me set up a thief-proof alarm system.

This car I was having built was a VN SS Commodore. I had it stripped down and rebuilt the way I wanted it. The engine was sent to my mechanic who just happened to hold the record for building the fastest Ute in Sydney. He blueprinted the engine, stroked it, fitted it with under the bonnet supercharger and just for that little bit extra he had nitro fitted. The paint guy stripped it back to bare metal and re-painted it a gloss black, and my upholster did the entire interior in soft grey leather. It had the best suspension fitted and of course the alarm system was unbeatable. There were no badges on the car and looking at it you wouldn't know what was under the hood, but when I put my foot down anyone could tell it wasn't stock. It was the perfect car for me. There was that incredible feeling of accomplishment when you have your own car built to your taste, to just how you want it. I had wanted to build my own car that way for as long as I could remember. I spent a fortune making it perfect for how I wanted it but every dime I spent on it was worth it. By now, you would have guessed that I was a car buff; I have a high taste in cars; only a few impressed me, and when I had seen and driven enough, I decided it was only right that I created one myself, one that would perfectly fit my taste.

So, on this morning I was discussing removing all locks on the car and making it remote control. I was walking up and down my lounge looking out to the water through my veranda when I got that gut feeling that has always guided my decisions throughout my life. As I spoke on the phone to the car thief, I walked over to my front door and looked out of the peephole. What I saw instantly put all my sensors on high alert and the rest of my body on auto drive: on the other side of my front, I saw about five plain-clothes police officers with sledgehammers and guns drawn. I slowly moved away from the peephole still talking to the car thief on the phone calmly, and at the same time getting rid of any drugs I had. This was bad, very bad. I was not prepared for something like this. But I chose to not panic. If the cops were coming for me it would still take them a couple of minutes before they arrived were organised; and if I were fast enough, I could get rid of anything incriminating before they hit. The first thing I had to make disappear was the drugs. First, I cleared the table of the coke there, then I went into the bedroom to get rid of a few wraps I had in the house. I thought about where to hide them, but I was not in the right state of mind to come up with any concrete idea. I thought about flushing them down the toilet but immediately dismissed the idea. The coke cost a fortune; I wouldn't want to do something that would make me later regret my decision. What if the cops had not come for me? There were still 2 other doors on either side of mine, that would mean that I had only panicked for nothing. And so, as I was still thinking about what to do next, an idea suddenly occurred to me. I went to the kitchen, stood on a stool and reached into the ceiling. I deposited the drugs there and quickly climbed back down. I knew it wasn't the most secure place to hide the drugs. If the police had really come to search my apartment for drugs it wouldn't take them much time to discover where I stashed them. I sincerely prayed they had not come for me. I tried to think about other reasons they might have made an appearance here, but I could not come up with anything. Every indication pointed to the fact that they had come for me. I knew I had slipped up really bad. I had acted carelessly, and my careless lifestyle had come back to bite me in the arse. But still, I tried to remain calm. If I appeared agitated before the cops that would give them enough reason to investigate me further. I must be smart about how to deal with them when they came knocking on my door.

But in my panicky state I had not gotten rid of all the drugs in the house; there were still a few left. I moved swiftly from one spot to the other collecting all the drugs in the house and surveying my surroundings at the same time. I knew that they hadn't yet covered the back of my unit that faced the river, and the windows facing a courtyard outside my kitchen were also clear. I started throwing the few remaining drugs out the window onto the roof facing me in the courtyard and then I tried throwing a few ounces over my balcony into the Glebe Foreshore. I was still talking to the car thief discussing the type of sound system I wanted fitted and at the same time doing a stock take in my head thinking did I get everything. Considering the seriousness of the situation, I think I acted calmly. I didn't spook the person at the other end of the phone into thinking there was something wrong. If by any chance someone had been studying me, they would only see someone speaking on phone and cleaning his apartment. Of course, what I was throwing out of the window might raise a few eyebrows but they wouldn't immediately assume that I was getting rid of drugs, because I was doing everything as calmly as I could. From experience, I had known that panicking might cause me to do something silly. I might even forget to get rid of a few drugs. I needed to keep my head straight; and that was exactly what I managed to do. The police would have a hard time connecting anything incriminating with me. I was sure I had done a good job in cleaning up my own mess.

I was still thinking if I hadn't made any error when the cops made a sudden appearance. I was searching around the room still looking for whatever incriminating might remain when they arrived. At that point all hell broke loose. One officer came running in shouting "police!" and waving a gun to my head.

My back was turned to them when they stepped in. I slowly put up my other hand that wasn't holding the phone and slowly turned to face them; this was not my first time of having an encounter with the police. Whenever they make an appearance that way, the best thing to do is to obey them by putting up your hands. But I could only raise one hand, the other was still holding the phone that was pressed against my ear. At that moment my recipient at the other end of the phone knew there was something wrong. He heard the scream of 'police' as loudly as I heard it, so he remained quiet. I expected that he would cancel the call but for some reason he didn't; I'd have to do it from my end. The one holding the gun was sweating and his hand was shaking. I could tell he was new at this, so I didn't do anything to spook him any further. Anything wrong from my part might cause him to involuntarily pull the trigger – I didn't need to put that kind of problem on myself. The situation wasn't bad enough to get killed over. I still had a lot of things to do and I didn't believe it was my time yet. When the police officer knocked the phone out of my hand, I told him to relax and that I was not going to do anything. As I was looking at him, trying to relax him a bit, I took in everything happening around me. Officer after officer was coming into my apartment. It was getting very crowded. They didn't even knock before stepping in. Things seemed to be more serious than I had thought. These people had come for business. It was either they had suspected me of crime due to the extravagant life I lived or someone had tipped them off about my drug business – either way, I knew things weren't looking good for me. The only thing I could hope for was that the police wouldn't find anything they could charge me with. If they found any trace of drugs in my apartment then I was really sunk.

To my utter surprise, I was handcuffed and sat down in my lounge. They didn't even find anything yet and they were already placing the bracelets on me. I was told I was under arrest but I didn't know what crime they were charging me with. It didn't seem like the visit was to search my apartment; they had come to arrest me outright. One officer in a suit started to read me my rights and told me where they were all from. I had the drug squad there, the crime commission and the club squad. He started explaining what they were looking for and how they were going to go about doing things. He explained that as they found items that they identified as items of interest, they would ask me about them, giving me an opportunity to explain what they were and if I owned them. These words seemed reasonable enough; I just didn't understand why they had to put me in handcuffs before they could do what they had come for. Did they think I was going to escape from them? How could I? They were a horde in my apartment. They had actually come to search the apartment after all; and the man in suit was explaining things to me in a polite manner. If I didn't know better, I would have thought he was looking out for my own interest; but I knew these police officers. They were sneaky men who could spin any yarn to put the ropes on you. He asked if I understood what he had been telling me and I reluctantly nodded yes. Perhaps the right thing for me to have done was to request for their search warrant or ask for a lawyer. But I didn't have a personal lawyer and I knew that the one the state would provide for me would be the lousiest one they could find. Besides, all these would only happen after I had been taken to their station, not when they were searching my apartment. There was really nothing I could do to stop them. It was a fact that I would just have to accept. I was under close scrutiny.

Since trying to calm the officer with the gun down I hadn't said a single word; I only gave a nod here and there. Well, there was really nothing much I could do in that situation. Since I was a young kid growing up on the streets of Marrickville and Dulwich Hill, I knew you never speak to cops. Even if you were innocent, they would always find a way to use your words against you, so I always stayed quiet. Usually, I don't even tell them my name, but these guys knew who I was; they probably knew what I had for breakfast that morning. As they were searching my apartment, I was still doing a stock take in my head trying to think if I missed anything. In my mind I was praying that they wouldn't have to search inside the kitchen ceiling; that would be the final nail in my coffin. Funny enough, that seemed to be the only thing I was worried about. Surely, if the police searched well, they would find other incriminating stuff in the house but nothing would trump the problem I would be in if they found the drugs. Discovering an unregistered ammunition could be as bad as the drugs but I knew I didn't possess any gun; I never really wanted to own a firearm. In that regard, I should put my mind at rest. But then again it was possible that some of the members who had been partying in my house might have forgotten a gun in my apartment without my knowledge. If such happened, I could be facing some really serious charges. Then suddenly I remembered the book with all the money owed and by who; it was the book that contained all the drug transactions I did. If the police came across it that would be as incriminating as discovering the drugs. I might just be in more of a serious pickle than I thought I was. What about other damning evidence that my mind did not even register at the moment? I wish I had known about the police visit a lot earlier. I wish I had known since yesterday; I would have done a thorough cleaning. But the police didn't always give notice when they were out to bust a suspect. They got me at a very bad time. All I could pray for was that they wouldn't find anything serious to charge me with.

Even though the details contained in the book were all in code I knew they would know what it was. But I couldn't do anything about it; it was too late to get rid of it. I was handcuffed already. Even if I wasn't there was no way I would be able to get rid of the book in the presence of the cops. As all this was going on the guy in the suit was still trying to talk to me. He was talking to me like he was trying to be my friend even though I wasn't paying any attention to him. At one point it got so annoying I broke my silence and said, "Look you could ask me if that's a wall there," indicating the wall beside me with my head, "I would not answer you until I speak to my lawyer first." This shut him up. Well, finally I was coming to my senses. I had made the officer know that there was no way he would be able to make me say things that would later be used against me. If he thought I was that dumb then he was gravely mistaken. I already knew so much about their tactics and only a few words from them would move me. I went back to being silent as the younger officers searched all the corners of my apartment. They wore gloves as they picked up objects, observed them and returned them to the same exact position they had been lifted. None of them gave me a glance; they were devoted to their jobs.

"If there is anything worth finding here," said the plain-clothed officer, "My men are going to find it."

I knew he was trying to get a reaction from me but I wasn't going to give him that luxury. I wanted to shrug indifferently at first but thought better of it. I didn't want to give him any response whatsoever. So, I remained unresponsive. Occasionally I would tell the cops to be careful whenever they picked up a delicate object but they acted as though I wasn't speaking to them. The first thing the cops came upon was the stash I had hidden in a small safe.

"Whose money is this?" the plain-clothed man asked me, flourishing the content of the safe.

"It's mine," I replied.

"How did you come across such a large sum of money?"

"It's not a large sum," I answered, "It's just a couple of thousand dollars."

"That's a large sum in my book," he said calmly. "How did you get the money?"

"I work as a security agent in a club. That money is my savings from the job."

"Why didn't you keep it in the bank?"

"It's my choice to put my money wherever I want to. Since when has that ever been a problem?"

"You say you're a security agent but that's not what I heard about you."

"What did you hear about me?" I demanded.

He stared at me for a moment and then looked away. He had no intention of engaging me in further discussion.

After four hours of them going through my apartment with me there and not finding anything worth their time I was taken to the cop shop to be charged. I considered myself incredibly lucky; even if I was going to be charged there was nothing really concrete to charge me for. Things would have turned out really bad for me if they had come across any ounce of the cocaine, or even the purchase book. I'm still surprised how they were unable to locate the book. I didn't even hide; it was there in plain sight and they didn't notice it. Perhaps they had seen it but didn't bother to check its content. Well, that was my luck. But since they wanted to charge me even though they didn't find any evidence in my house, then the obvious must have happened. It seems as though I had been under surveillance for six months and they already had enough to charge me with, but by the looks on some of their faces they expected much more – they had come to get the last piece of nail that would permanently shut me in my coffin, but unfortunately for them they came up short. Whatever they would be charging me for now was most probably weak. It wasn't until the next day they discovered some of the drugs I had disposed of; not much but it was something. That was the final blow. When I had thought I was home free, the cops came up with a treasure. I hadn't thought that they would search the surrounding areas too. If I had known I wouldn't have thrown the drugs out as I did. There was still enough space in my ceiling to stash them. But because of the heat of the moment, I wasn't exactly thinking straight 100% - now my action had returned to bite me in the tail. At this juncture, I didn't need a priest to inform me that I was in serious trouble. I remember one of the cops came into the cop shop with a big smile on his face and he went out of his way to let me know they found my drugs. If only he knew. If I wasn't experienced, I would have shown reaction and panicked, but I remained emotionless; I didn't want to give them any impression that I understood what they were talking about. But I still could not stop thinking about the quantity of the drugs they had found. But does quantity matter? What they needed was the right evidence, no matter how minuscule. I guessed that was what they had been searching for to finally bring me down. Whichever the case might be, I gave myself the consolation that at least they hadn't found the drugs in my apartment. A good lawyer could argue it out.

I got processed, charged and sent to jail at Long Bay. I was only there for three days before my lawyer got bail for me. The restrictions were a bit harsh for what they had found but the police prosecutor said there would be more charges once all the evidence was processed, meaning all the recordings from six months of audio and video surveillance. If that was the case, I might just be looking at a very long time in jail eventually. I wondered how they were able to get audio surveillance on me. Had they bugged my apartment when I wasn't around? Had they been listening to every conversation I had with people. When all the reality slowly occurred to me, I began to sweat. If that was the case, I might not be the only one going to jail, a lot of other people might just be jailed too. It was hard to imagine that the police would bring down the rest of my friends because I had been sloppy. It would be a disgrace on my part. What about video surveillance? If the police put their minds on something, they are usually dedicated to getting desired result. The videos could even be more damning than the audio evidence. They might have tailed me to where I supplied my customers coke and stuff. Video evidence must have captured me snorting with a couple of other people from my club. It seemed like there was no way I would be able to wring myself off this one. Not even the best lawyers in the world might be able to keep me from going to jail. At this point, I didn't really worry about going to jail; what concerned me was the people that would be jailed on my account. I couldn't have that kind of thing on my conscience. My reputation would be ruined if words got out that others had been jailed because I got sloppy; I would automatically lose my respect in the street. So, I got bail for $10,000 security and had to report every day. Bear and Turk picked me up and took me back to the Glebe apartment. As we were returning to the apartment, I looked at Bear and Turk and wondered if they were under police surveillance too. I wondered how much the police must have had on them. I thought about going underground; but that was close to impossible now. I was already marked; and as soon as I refuse to report on a day, every law enforcement agency in the country would be searching for me. I knew I was in a trap now; there was no way for me to escape. I had no choice but to wait for the final verdict. As soon as I walked in, I could see the extent of their destruction. I looked around to see if they missed anything and I couldn't believe it, on top of my fridge were three grams of pure coke.

You see when you get a kilo or more you blend a handful of rock coke and powder from the bottom of the bag. Once it's all blended together you weigh one gram of it and cook it back to pure oil, which hardens up once removed from the bicarb and water. You then weigh that and see what's left after all the impurities are gone. So, if you cook up one gram and end up with 0.8 of a gram you know it's 80% pure. If you get back 0.9 of a gram then you know that's as pure as you can get processed coke for snorting. There are others who cook it back to smoke it but that's as addictive as shooting it up. In fact, that's what they call freebasing it. In the US it's called "crack" and it's very addictive. I have always stayed away from that. I would usually save all the grams I cooked to check the purity and give them to the good customers who bought a lot from me. But not this time. I crushed up one of the rocks and snorted it. It was the last time I took coke.

Maybe I shouldn't have explained the process of cooking up coke; my intention isn't to put crazy ideas in the heads of people, I just don't want to leave any detail unexplained. Well, to hell with it, there is nothing new in what I'm explaining. People from the street are already cooking coke on the regular. And these days, nothing is hidden anymore. If you don't read about it in this book, you will come across it someday when surfing the internet. It's no longer a big deal. I always believe that if you've got to do something you've got to do it right, and in the best way. Mediocrity is not a word in my lexicon. It is often hard to really get pure coke in the streets. From experience there are a lot of users who would snort anything as long as it made them high; they didn't always care whether it was pure or not. Only the elites (which were the people I dealt with) wanted pure unadulterated drugs, and they had the money to pay for them. They wouldn't take the cheap chaff the common users usually took. I have seen a lot of dealers on street corners selling poor products to ignorant users who were only desperate to have something to snort up their nostrils or shot into their bloodstream through syringes. Like I said, I am not a fan of needles. I don't cook my coke to free base it; I am contented with snorting it and feeling its effect straight up. I wasn't going to allow myself to become so pathetic that I would sport a lot of needle holes on my body. Besides, if the people I dealt with found such holes on one's body, there wouldn't be anything you would say to convince them otherwise about their theory of you.

The next day I picked up the Commodore and started tying up some loose ends; I knew all I was doing was damage control now, but I couldn't just sit down and do nothing. If I could reduce the extent of the damage, then I should. The raid had cost me a lot but not everything. I still had most the money, so I collected as I needed it. The crime commission took a 930 Turbo Porsche, my fat boy, a new Honda, $30,000 cash and a further $30,000 in gold. I was lucky because they didn't know about the beast I was having built and they had no way of recovering all the money. They also took my boat; they took it from Cabarita Point and dry-docked it in Balmain.

They wanted to leave me as powerless as possible. Even if I wanted to abscond, I was basically broke. There was no way I could escape if I had no money to pay for all the requirements. I guessed that was their reason for taking my property. I always wonder what they would do with all they had seized. Well, if I won the case against me (which was highly, highly unlikely) they would have no choice but to return everything they had taken. I should kiss all that stuff goodbyes anyway. I can't think of any way I could win this case. I would have to make do with the little I had left. I started by collecting from all those who owed me. If I had known that this was how things were going to eventually turn out, I would have sold off all those things they took. I wouldn't even have bought the boat. I was just about enjoying it when the police made their sensational appearance. Well, at this point, all I could hope for was to stay out of jail. If I could somehow be free, in no time I would get back all that I had lost. I might even become bigger and, of course, I would be a lot more careful with the way I would live my life. I would refrain from being excessively flamboyant. It would be a hard thing to do but I must learn. Well, I might just be wishing things that might not come to pass. It was certain that I was going to jail. I suppose what I should be thinking about was how I would plan when I would come out of jail. Then again, I couldn't imagine how long I would spend in jail. It might really be a long time. My fear was that I would become an old man when I eventually come out. I was in great trouble. I didn't imagine that this was going to be my plight. I was feeling sorry for myself. Prison isn't a nice place for anyone to be – well, here I am.

Things made a great turn a couple of days after they had seized the boat. It must have been costing them a fortune because after one week they realized payments were being made on it and they couldn't sell it, so they were calling my lawyers every day to try and get me to pick up the boat. If they could sell it, they would have, but they couldn't. It was not pretty that they were paying for something that was entirely useless to them. Even if I didn't think that this was how things would turn out to be for them. They wanted to continue keeping it, but they didn't want to pay a dime for its maintenance; they asked me to pay for the dry-docking. I knew at this point, I had them by the balls. Even if it was a fleeting victory, it was still a victory nonetheless. It was cool having an advantage over those bastards. I wasn't going to pay for the dry-docking as long as the boat was still under their care. If they wanted me to take care of the payment, then they had to release it back. When my lawyers explained the situation to me, I laughed hard. I admit, I felt a little bit better about that; it wasn't every time you had the police in a corner. I told my lawyers to tell them to put it back exactly where they took it from and after two weeks they did. They couldn't bear to pay further for it.

I couldn't go back to my apartment after it was raided so I stayed in hotels every night; even if I could, I wouldn't want to go back to that place. It might be crawling with surveillance gadgets and what-have-you; I didn't want to give the police any more evidence to add for the ones already compiled against me. At first, I stayed in The Novotel in the City but after one month of that I thought I better stop spending like I was. I also started to spend more time with Jane who was already my girlfriend, and eventually moved into a flat in Bondi with Jane and her daughter. With Jane in my life, I was ready to be serious about my life. I saw myself planning the future with Jane and her daughter. To be honest, Jane was the girl of my dreams; she was everything I desired in a woman. And I cared about her daughter as much as I cared about her. I didn't know the story about the father of the girl; but I supposed he was an irresponsible fellow. Who in his right senses would get someone like Jane pregnant and then abscond? It was hard to believe. Perhaps the father of the girl was dead or something. Whatever the case might be, I was ready to always be there for Jane, of course that was if I didn't eventually end up in jail. Jane herself was an understanding woman. She knew everything about my business, and she supported me wholeheartedly. She was an outstanding woman. At times I would wonder what she saw in me that made her agree to be my girlfriend. And moving into a new apartment with her and her daughter could be one of the best decisions I had ever made. I was starting a family with her and I didn't regret my decision one bit.

Because I knew that the police were watching my every step now, I stopped all drug-related business but continued my wild ways, even though I was in a relationship again. I didn't do what I had done in the past, meaning I didn't try to be someone I wasn't. I told Jane this is what I am like, if you can handle it, I will give this a go. She accepted me and my lifestyle. She continued to work as a stripper, and I continued to go away for three and four days in a row partying with the club and she never asked one question.

I didn't ask questions about her stripping business either. I knew in her kind of business she might need to flirt with some men and I had made my peace with that. I was ready to accept Jane for who she was, just as she had accepted me for who I was too. We both agreed that the companionship was most important. I was free to sleep with as many girls as I wanted, but none of them would take the spot of Jane in my heart. I liked the fact that Jane didn't try to meddle in any of my business. We both knew our lanes and we stayed there. It was a case of mutual respect; she respected my space and I respected hers in return. It was like living with a mate. I had never tried having a relationship this way, but it was working. The most important thing was that we understood each other perfectly well. We only had to look in each other's eyes and we would know what the other person was thinking. Every moment we had sex it was always glorious. Sex with Jane was always like fine wine; there would be something new every time, like I was getting to know more about her personality through sex; I don't know if I'm making sense right now. Anyway, my home was my home and the club house was the place where I would party. I had gotten to that stage where I didn't bring the business of the club house to the house. I had learnt my lessons from the last raid. I didn't trust the police to not have bugged even the new apartment I shared with Jane. When it came to investigations, there was no line the police would not cross. And so, everything related to the club stayed in the club. I even hardly received or made phone calls at home.

City Chapter Life

One day Jane asked me to talk to a young guy she knew who worked as a bouncer at the Black Market. His name was John and he kept on asking Jane about getting an introduction. He already had a Harley and was covered in tattoos, plus like many doormen in the city he loved to work out. But what he loved more was the bikie lifestyle. So, I agreed to talk to him and I liked him straight away. He wasn't too loud and only spoke when something needed to be said. I nommed him up to the city chapter. It was funny that now I could nom people up. It was just like yesterday when Bear was trying to nom me too up into the Rebel. In John, I saw a younger version of myself. He was the picture of the kind of people I liked associating myself with. He might be covered in tattoos and look rough but, John was an intelligent fellow. He didn't just work out too, he could hold himself in a brawl. It wasn't like I had seen him fight anyone before; but instincts always tell these things. You could work out a person by the way they act and you would be able to determine what they can or cannot do. Looking at John, I knew he was not a pussy; he was no coward – and that was the kind of person needed in the Rebels. We needed more of people with his kind of spirit, his passion. He had a likeable character; everyone who met him would immediately like him at first sight, and the way he would relate with the person would even make the person like him more. Even as a nom, he was already assuming a stance of authority. His fellow noms often looked up to him for advice and stuff, and John was always ready to help. He had the spirit of the brotherhood. He also would not discriminate against anyone. He respected people's beliefs and ideas, just like he would want people to respect his own beliefs in return. John hardly screamed or made expletives. He was often calm and collected. He could also party as hard as anyone, and he was respectful towards people who were more superior to him. On that note, I couldn't say we shared anything in common. I remember that in my nomming days I was rebellious towards people more superior to me. I cut a lot of corners during my nomming days; but John wasn't doing that – he was doing everything by the book. He would serve drinks and clean up after every party. He didn't mind since he knew that all these were only going to go on for 12 months. He was patient, he was level-headed. He didn't cause any chaos and he had no bad blood with any nom or member. He was courteous to everybody, and he always received the same courtesy in return.

Here is what the rest of the city chapter was like. There was Bear, a 10-year member, as the President. Then there was Harry, another 10-year member, who was a very talented boxer and tattooist, and brought with him a lot of military experience. Harry was Vice President, then there was our Sergeant-of-Arms, Frank. Frank wasn't a big man but what he lacked in size did not in any way take away from his animal instinct and strength. Everyone who knew Frank would avoid getting in trouble with him. A lot of people who had underestimated him because of his size had suffered some permanent damage to their bodies.

When Frank was based in Bringelly, he would go to Liverpool methadone clinic early in the morning after a night of drinking and stand in front of the door not letting anyone go in for their dose. I had heard about it but thought it was just a rumour until I witnessed it myself. One night after partying at Bringelly one of the members said "Come with me and have a look at something." I didn't know where we were going but I jumped into his car and he drove me to the methadone clinic in Liverpool and there was Frank in his colours with his bike next to him standing in front of the clinic with a line of addicts in front of him begging him to let them in to get their dose. But Frank would not budge, and no one tried to get past him because he grew up in the area and already had a reputation of being a hard man. One time Frank had a fight with a group of men in the car park of a shopping centre, and after beating the crap out of two of the guys who started it, he ripped the car door off its hinges to get to the driver. That was Frank. Those guys could not believe their eyes when they saw Frank use his bare hands to rip out the door. When Frank got to the driver, he dragged the man out and holding him firmly by the scruff of his shirt, lifted him in the air, totally off his feet as if he was a pillow. Then he tossed the driver away like a kitten. The man crashed into something hard and remained there. Whenever Frank was on a roll like that, no one would dare try to stop him. All anyone could do was to watch. Eventually Frank's anger would simmer down and he would become himself. Whenever he was upset like that, it was always like a beast had taken possession of him because of the superhuman strength he often exhibited. But when he became calm, he would return to that little guy people often underestimated. And in that calm state, he could even have a couple of drinks with the people he had just fought. Frank harboured no resentment against anyone; he was just a man who firmly stuck to his principles.

Then there was Turk. Turk was our Treasurer and completely different from everyone else in our chapter. Turk had his colours as long as me but hung around the club much longer than me. He didn't drink, didn't take drugs and didn't sleep around once he met his wife; not your usual bikie but that's what made us different from other bike clubs. Because you are a bikie does not mean you have to live your life a certain way. You are in control of your own life; no one would tell you this is the way you must live because you're a bikie. Turk was one of the few members who chose to be absolutely pure. Even in the midst of all the drinking, snorting and whoring around, these individuals like this would not engage in any of the aforementioned. They were contented with the way they were living their simple life. They joined the bikie club because of their love for motorcycles and the camaraderie of the membership. Some joined just because being a bikie made them look somewhat tough, even though they had no tough bones in their bodies. But of course, we didn't just take anybody; anyone who would join the club must have a certain merit. If you are not physically solid then you must be intellectually strong; you must bring something to the table. We have many family men, even grandparents in the club, and they all went through the nomming process. It doesn't matter what your age is you must pass through a certain level before getting to another level. That's just how it is – equality at all level. However, like me, if you know your way about boycotting some of the processes without attracting too much attention to yourself, then you are free to try. Each member respected the space of another member; no bikie would go around screwing the wife of another bikie, it was totally unacceptable. Anyone who does that will immediately be cut off from the club; it would definitely be a great disgrace for a member to be disowned by his own club. Everyone was an individual and Turk was one of the most loyal men I ever met; he knew his place in the club and he stuck to it. He never ventured to do what was beyond his level; and he was courteous to everyone around. He was the kind of guy anyone could tell a secret and no third party would hear about it, no matter how grave the secret might be. Turk was so trustworthy that some members who didn't like using the bank – and who didn't fancy keeping money in their houses too – would seek out Turk and give him their money to keep for them. Turk was always upstanding; he always came through whenever they needed their money. The other three members to make up the city chapter were Nevil, Agro and myself. John was our nom. That was the city chapter.

Life went on. Jane left Dancers so she could get a job more suitable to our new setup so she started working in a gentleman's restaurant in the city. That way she could work while her daughter was at school. It was actually a great relief to me to know that she was not going to be stripping for anyone again. Her daughter was growing up; it was high time she left the stripping business and delved into something more respectable. It was better that she was working in the day and she would not have to abandon her daughter every night to just go and strip herself naked at Dancers. The other good thing was that Reese's school was directly across the road from our flat. I could give her a little wave from my room when she was out in the playground. Whenever I was home during school hours, I was always looking through my window to the playground of the school, watching over her. And when the school closed and I was around, I would volunteer to go pick her up from school. Like I said, the school was just across the road from us but still I always wanted to pick her up; I was never tired of doing that. Every time I went to pick her like that, Reese was always complaining that I was treating her like a little girl.

"I can come home on my own," she would complain, "I'm not a baby anymore."

"You'll always be a baby to me, darling," I would reply to her and she would squeeze her face together in displeasure.

"Mommy always allows me to come home on my own," she would say.

"Well, I'll tell mommy to never do that again."

Her eyes would open wide and she would say, "Oh no, you wouldn't!"

Of course, I wouldn't, I was only messing with her. But unlike Jane I couldn't sit around and watch her cross the road herself. Something terrible might happen; she might be knocked down by a careless driver. Even though she was not mine by blood, I loved Reese as much as I would have loved my own child. I couldn't bear imagine anything bad happening to her. She was too innocent to be hurt. I had sworn to always protect Jane and her daughter, and I wasn't looking forward to breaking my promise to them. As it was, Jane and Reese were the most important people of my life; there was nothing I wouldn't do for those two women. If I lost them, I had no idea how I was going to survive it. They had become a very important part of my life; they brought light into the dark tunnels of my life. They were my everything. I had put everything in place that if I died today, Jane and her daughter would be set for life – everything I own would go to them.

Through the week our lives were as normal as they could be and, on the weekends, when Reese stayed at her dad's family home, we would have people over. Oh, I must tell you that I later learnt about Reese's father. He was not married to Jane; she got pregnant to him when they were only dating. Now he always paid for child support and stuff, and the child was often taken to pay her father's family a visit; and she was always accepted as a part of the family. Reese was loved by everybody – who wouldn't have loved such an incredible girl. She was intelligent and very smart. Wherever she went, she was always the centre-point of the place, even as young as she was. Many had said that Reese would grow up to become very successful. I couldn't argue with that; of course, Reese had the gift of becoming exactly that. So, each time Reese left the house we would have a party at the apartment, and we could drink and take drugs as much as we wanted without having to worry that there was a child in the house. When John needed a place to stay, we allowed him to stay in the house with us. He was given a spare room where he could always stay. He would work as a bouncer at night in various clubs in the City and sleep all day in the spare room. Through the week he wasn't allowed to bring any girls over because we had a young girl living with us now and my upbringing made me very protective of her. Little girls were quick to catch stuff; if John started bringing girls to the room, Reese's mind might be corrupt. I didn't want the innocent child to grow up into one of those messed up girls in the street. She didn't have to grow up to do the same jobs her mother did to survive. She deserved a lot better than that. It would only take a moment of seeing John on top of another lady for her mind to be scarred forever. So, we took every precaution and forbade John from entertaining any woman in the house. He seemed to understand our angle perfectly well too and he agreed to abide by the rules. Besides, there were hundreds of places he could take any woman to. He was a bouncer anyway; he would have knowledge of a lot of spots to take his catch to. John respected me a lot; I knew he was not going to do anything to jeopardize his stay in our apartment. He was very true to his words; he didn't bring in any woman to the house. Sometimes he would not come home at all; I guessed that was because he would have to spend the night with some of the girls he had picked up. It was only a matter of time before he got his own apartment.

From day one Reese was like my own daughter, since I never had my own kids. Because of the lifestyle I lived and my upbringing – to me it was always one or the other, settle down and start a family or live hard and fast and die young – I never saw my life going past 30. So, this was all new to me. I matched up both of my lives into one and it was working.

I continued to do the family thing through the week and the bikie thing on the weekends, occasionally going on a run for a week. But everything else to do with selling drugs or the Cross was over. I had to start getting all my ducks in a row before my court case came up. I now felt responsible for Jane and Reese so I wanted to make sure they would be alright when I was gone.

I started spending a lot of time with an accountant from Canberra called Frank. He had some trouble with our boys in the Canberra chapters, so I bailed him out and in return he showed me how all the politicians in Canberra made their money. It was like pulling money out of thin air and it was legal as far as I could tell, so I started setting up a company with him and the plan was in about a year we could pull out about $20 million from this company. It was incredible; this was like gold mine. It simply meant that I would not have to do anything illegal, and I might be making as much as I was making from selling drugs. The deal was juicy in the extreme. At first it sounded too good to be true; I initially suspected him of trying to defraud me so I stepped back a little bit. I wasn't going to push in my money to something I wasn't entirely sure of, but Frank assured me it was real.

So, things went along slowly. Jane and I spent more and more time with Frank and his girl. Frank would do one of his accounting tricks every now and then and put $10,000 in my pockets from thin air; that plus all the money owed to me from drug debts and I was still living comfortably. It was great way to make cool hard cash; and I looked forward to making as much as I could before the opportunity closed. Besides, the dates of my court cases were approaching; I might be shipped away to prison before I got the chance to make enough to take good care of Jane and Reese. I tried to speed up the account but Frank told me that was not the way things worked; I would have to be patient with things. The most incredible aspect was that this money seemed to come from thin air indeed, I couldn't tell where it had come from. I didn't know what the business was – just knew that money was coming in.

I didn't need the boat anymore so I passed it on to another member from Queensland. He paid me $30,000 to take over the payments and he took it up to Airlie Beach. I remember meeting him there to finalize everything and making a weekend of it. I invited the original owner of the boat, Steve, as my guest and another member from the Surfers Paradise chapter. His name was Ahmed. The transitioning of the boat was painful to imagine. Even though I knew I didn't need it anymore, it wasn't like I didn't want it. Having it passed on to someone else pulled at my heart. I had thought I was going to do incredible things with the boat; well, there were other better things to do. I held my last party on the boat and invited a lot of friends. The party was wild as usual; the police were still watching my every move. They were waiting for me to slip off so that they could finally close in on my fate and move on to the next person of interest. Even though I knew that the police had some evidence they would use against me during my hearing, I still felt like they hadn't gotten enough, and they were looking to me to make them complete everything they would need to destroy me. I had to be extremely careful. I later learnt that there were some of the guests who came with their own coke but did things discreetly. They locked themselves somewhere and lined up what they had. After that, they cleaned their nose and appeared back among the crowd. Thankfully, nobody suspected anyone of anything. If it had been discovered that someone lined up at my party, my situation might become worse. But it wouldn't mean much since the drug was not found with me. There was no way I could have known that someone was coming to my party with drugs. It was something that could very well be argued in court. But fortunately, something like that was not noticed. At the end of the party, I handed all the documents belonging to the boat to the new owner. At least the money I made from selling it could go a long way in making my family comfortable. And I hope that this new owner would have much fun as I did.

We all flew into Airlie Beach then caught another charter to Hamilton Island. Once there we made reservations at a resort and went to our rooms to rest and get ready for the night. When I got to my room, I realized I left my bag with all my clothes and the $30,000 in cash at the travel agency we made the bookings at. When I told Steve and Ahmed, I lost my bag with $30,000 in it they were more distressed than me. They wanted to turn Hamilton Island upside down until we found it, but I had already accepted I had lost it for good. But in order to get them off my back we retraced our steps and believe it or not the bag with the $30,000 was still where I left it. It was incredible that we still found the bag there. $30,000 was a large sum of money and anyone who found it would have been very comfortable, but no one took interest in the bag.

Perhaps if I had fully accepted that I had lost the money and not bothered to come back for it, someone who really needed it would have taken it; but as it turned out, no one was worthy of the money. I was glad to find the money intact. $30,000 might not mean so much to me but it was a great addition to my wealth. Besides the money, there were other valuable items and documents contained in the bag of money so in truth was relieved I found it.

After that bit of luck, I knew it was my shout all weekend. Ahmed and I ran amuck for two days and nights. We were driving these little golf carts all over the island because there was no other way of transport. We drove them to every drinking establishment on the island and when I say "we drove them to" I mean we actually drove through the swinging doors and right up to the bar to order our drinks. Eventually they got sick of us and got island security to talk to us, but I wasn't having any of it. No one was taking my golf buggy off me. I was willing to drive it off the pier rather than hand it over, and I did. With the island security running up behind us we went straight for a pier and drove them off. It was a crazy thing to do; even the securities looked at us as if a screw had gone lose in our domes. We were too glad to have the carts over the piers than to have them impounded by the security officers.

As Ahmed and I swam off, we could see security men on their walkie-talkies. We knew then the party was over; now the security officials would be on our case; there was no point trying to continue the party anymore. We went back to our accommodations, gathered all our belongings, told Steve that Ahmed and I had to split, and we were off.

First, I tried to get a private 2-seater plane to fly us back to the mainland, but they were booked out. We thought if we could at least get off Hamilton then we'd be halfway there. So, we got on this ferry full of tourists and sat there as we slowly moved away from the Wharf. Once we were far enough from the island, Ahmed started playing up again. He had confiscated the microphone from the guy explaining all of North Queensland's wonders and started telling jokes. At one point he tried to get a conga line going. It was hilarious and the tourists didn't mind it either. The tourist guide wasn't too happy but at least we gave him a story to tell his grandchildren one day, the day his ship was taken over by a club of unruly bikies. Perhaps when his grandchildren hear the story, they would want to become bikies too. But I trust the tourist guide to paint us in the darkest colour before his kids. Maybe this was how we had always been painted; as unruly and violent criminals riding around towns in their big bikes, for we suffered a lot of discrimination among people. The society generally believes that no good can come from a club of motorcycle-riding hooligans; but we were ready to change their impression about us only if they would give us the chance, but they don't. Because we drink, smoke, take drugs and party all night we have nothing else to think about. That's not true, not at all true. As a matter of fact, we have various professionals in various fields these people are respected and revered in the society whenever they were not in their usual bikie colours. We live in a world where you are judged by your appearance, not by your actions. A known serial killer may be respected provided he wears his suit and knots his tie. It's a crazy world we live in. Well, we never cared about the impression people may have about us – I don't care either. I do things based on the standards I place on myself, not what the society places on me.

When we got off the ferry, I found a pilot willing to fly us to Airlie Beach. We didn't play up on the plane, but I do remember asking the pilot if he could do a loop the loop. He reckoned he could but wouldn't prove it. If I had persuaded him further he might have done it. But somehow, he thought that was too dangerous a risk. What if he couldn't do it and ended up plunging us down to earth uncontrollably? The dumb stuff we could do on a plane was limited. Once back at Airlie Beach, Ahmed and I continued to drink and cause mischief. I remember at one point we were running in and out of backyards and Ahmed pushed me into a pool; it was the pool of total strangers; it belonged to a family we knew nothing about. Fortunately for us, no one came out to chase us away or anything. I guessed the family was not at home at that time. If they were and knew what was going on, they might have called the police. Looking at our sizes and appearances, they wouldn't want to face us directly. They would think they were being attacked. I don't remember why we were running or why he pushed me in but when he put his hand out to help me out of the water I remember trying to pull him in. But there was no chance of that. Ahmed had about 50kg on me. He just shook me off and I fell back in; I could remember how he had laughed at me as I fell. One thing about Ahmed is that he knows how to have fun and enjoy it. He could laugh hard at the slightest funny thing. Sometimes some people had underestimated him because he could laugh easily, and because of his cheerful nature. But I'm telling you, Ahmed is not a man you can cross. He's not the kind of person you can display your masculinity with. He rarely gets angry, granted, but when he is, he's a mad bull, and he is capable of causing some irreparable damage on you if you're not careful around him. After that we went and had some takeaway chips and that was the end of my Hamilton Island experience.

When I got back home, I found that my car was gone. That didn't worry me because ever since John moved in with us, I would let him use the beast to run errands. But he was getting too comfortable taking it just to impress women, so a couple of weeks after getting back I went and saw a friend of mine who owned a car yard. I asked him to find me the smallest street legal car he could find. I thought he would come back with a Mini Minor but he came through for me with something better. I think it was a Fiat Bambino. When you compare it to a mini, the mini looks like a limo. My mate at the car yard wanted to know what I was going to do with it, so I told him my nom needs his own car. That's when he fell over. You see my mate at the car yard had met my nom John and knew he was bigger than the Bambino. In fact, John could have probably worn the Bambino as a backpack. But he had already given me the Bambino and there was no going back. He would have loved to replace the Bambino with a Mini but I didn't allow that; the Bambino was perfect; I wouldn't have it any other way now.

But I needed to teach the nom a lesson: if he likes something, he will need to work to get it; if you just use other people's things when you can you don't move forward, you just stand still. I had the Bambino dropped off at our place. My unit was on a one-lane street, so I had it parked on the school side of the road directly under my bedroom window. It was there for about three days. No one asked about it or even mentioned it; it was of too low standard for anyone to use, especially for John. He didn't know I had got the car for him I was waiting for the time he would need to use a car.

Then John had a date with a Penthouse Pet, so he asked for the keys in his own shy way, as he had always asked in the past. I knew he was asking to use the beast but I wasn't going to allow that. The Bambino would not rot away where I put it; I had bought it for John and so he had to use it. This was what I had been waiting for; I had been waiting for him to ask for my car. I went to the bedroom, got the key for the Bambino and gave it to him. I didn't even look at his face to check his emotion. If he didn't want the car, he shouldn't desire another.

He looked at the key in his hand and then he looked at me waiting for an explanation; I gave him no explanation; the key was self-explanatory. He knew the beast had no keys. It was all operated by remote control and he wasn't holding a remote control.

"What is this?" he asked in disgust. I knew he already knew that I had given him the key to the Bambino, so I refused to respond to him.

"This isn't the key to the beast. Is this a joke or something?" he said again.

Okay, that was the word that pissed me off. He didn't even appreciate my effort that I got him a car in the first place. I wouldn't take that kind of tone from him. Besides he was living under my roof; he had to respect me and my rules if he still wanted to continue staying in my house. It was not like I had any personal grudge against him in the past or anything but I needed to let him remember his place in the house. I wouldn't allow him to make me inconvenient because I had chosen to accept him in my house – and hell, I wouldn't be talk to in that way. Like I already said, I liked John a lot but sometimes you've got to show tough love to the people you like so that they wouldn't get too comfortable to the extent that they begin to disrespect you.

So, I told him I got him his own car and that's when his expression changed from confused to excited; well, as excited as John ever showed. He never really expressed much emotion. He always had a serious and an annoyed expression on his face, but this one time I could see the beginning of a smile on his face. I didn't know whether to blame myself for making that statement or not. I couldn't really read any meaning to that smile he had plastered on his face. I had expected him to be angry. I had expected that we would scream expletives on each other, walk away in anger and them make up in the night by smoking some joints or having a drink. This smile was not the emotion I had expected of him. I tried to study his eyes to really know what his feelings were, but I was confused. All I could remember about his emotions was carrying an angry face; this particular one was new to me. I didn't know how to react to it.

He asked me where it was. Then I understood what his expression meant. He was genuinely happy by that smile;

I couldn't believe that he had not noticed the Bambino. Then my usual naughty thoughts crossed my mind. I was going to have fun with him. I tried to keep the smile off my face as I replied him. I told him it's parked out front. Then he asked what it was. Here I would have simply told him what I got him and I would have revelled in his horror but I didn't want to have the fun alone. I told him to go downstairs and I would point it out to him from my window. As soon as he was out the door, I grabbed Jane, just barely holding back my laughter. Jane knew straight away I was up to something; I had done a lot of pranks on her and in her presence to guess that I was being terrible again. I remember her saying "what did you do" in a half-worried way but I didn't say anything to her. I just guided her to our bedroom window and waited for John to get downstairs. Once he was out on the street, he looked up at us and I pointed out the Bambino to him. Again, no expression from him but I knew he was shattered; he was rigid there for a moment as he stared at the piece of junk. I knew what was going through his mind and I almost laughed out loud. He was most probably what people would say when they saw him driving around in a Bambino. I was at the window pissing myself laughing and Jane was just holding back her laughs by slapping me on the arms and saying, "you *are* terrible." Indeed, I was terrible. I was laughing so hard that I had snort coming out of my nose and tears from my eyes. John remained staring at the car for a while; he was debating within himself whether to accept the gift or just walk away. This sight of him confused about what to do tore me to pieces; I damn near peed myself that day. It was too funny to imagine. I tried to make my laughter as silent as possible but it was impossible for me to keep it down. I could swear that John heard me laugh at him, but he showed no reaction against that. Of course, he knew me not to be vindictive; he knew I was just having a laugh; he knew that I was not really mocking him. I was sure he took no offence at my laughter. Besides, he was just too shocked to take any offence at anything; he was just staring at the car with an unbelievable expression. If looks could change things, his look would have transformed the car into the best car in the world; but unfortunately for him nothing of such exists in this reality.

John still got in the car and – JUST – took off. He wasn't going to miss his date with a Penthouse Pet. He was just going to her place, so he didn't care how he got there just as long as he got there. The next time I saw him was a few days later when he came out of his room. I asked where the Bambino was. I saw that smile again, just letting me know I got him good and he appreciated my joke. That was one thing about John; he was just like me; he harboured no resentment. He understood that I was only messing around; he had no hatred for that. He wasn't angry; he was simply shocked by my action. So, he told me the story: he had to work after seeing the Penthouse Pet so he drove the Bambino to the Blackmarket and parked it across the road in the petrol station car park. When he finished his shift, he got into it and tried to get it started but it wouldn't start. He explained to me how all the other bouncers from the Blackmarket saw him get into the Bambino and try to start it. He told me how one staff member called another and so on until there were about eight staff members all around him laughing at him, half in half out of the car, trying to start it. Eventually a few of his colleagues told him to get in and try clutching it. They pushed him for two blocks before he got the shits at them pissing themselves laughing at him while pushing. He parked the car and caught a cab home. I was laughing so hard as he told me this story. I could imagine how hard those people who saw him with the car were laughing. And they even made things worse by trying to push him forward in the car. The final killing stroke was his decision to abandon the car. He felt he had had enough of the humiliation – that was exactly what I would have done too. Oh man, I laughed hard enough to cause a stomach ache. I was bent over as I laughed. That was an incredible piece of hilarious news.

I did end up picking it up again; I wouldn't abandon it there, of course. It would still be a lot useful. I was going to teach Jane how to drive again before I got her a proper car but she wouldn't get into it too. Even she knew that the Bambino was not worthy of a car to drive, or to learn how to drive in the first place. So, the car remained parked for a long time; no one went near it. I think John tried to use it one more time before it broke two streets away and that's where it stayed. I didn't bother to take it this time around; I was finally done with it. The Bambino was a useless car and it had played its part.

After that John ended up using the Fixer's car; he was lucky enough to find a replacement. Perhaps if he had not had any choice he would have gone back to where he abandoned the Bambino. Well, he was in the Fixer's grace. All he had to do was drive him around at night if he needed to go anywhere, and he was allowed to use it whenever he wanted, which was fine with him and the Fixer, and, of course, it was fine with me too, as long as he didn't have to make use of my beast. I wouldn't allow him to use that, not for anything. I would rather get him a Mini rather than allow him to drive around and carry girls with my beast. My lesson to try and make him get his own toys didn't work; I had sat him down a couple of times and told him he could get his shit together and get his own things. He would always listen to me attentively every time but he never took any step to following my advice. He seemed he was very comfortable about depending on other people for a living. As long as he had a place to sleep or food in his stomach, he was good. That was the difference between John and me; I would not settle to depend on other people for my own survival; I am a man who works for my own thing and get whatever I want myself. I wasn't wired to be a nuisance to other people. John was making enough money to be comfortable with himself but he had poor money management skill. I know I'm not one to give advice about savings and stuff but I can give good advice about personal discipline. If you can discipline yourself and stay off some pleasure, you will achieve your goals. That was the same thing I had been preaching to John over and over again, but they always seemed to fly over his head. If he needed anything, he could always depend on close associates to come through for him. He just found someone else he could borrow a good car from, and he was good; life was once again normal. I didn't understand why he wasn't interested in having his own stuff, but I accepted it. That's just how he was and far be it from me to try and change anyone. I would always share my knowledge with him but it was up to him if he wanted to use it. So, life was good. In fact, I had stopped trying to convince him to do what he wasn't ready to do. He was a stubborn guy, that's John. If he wasn't interested in anything, nothing would make him show interest. Well, live and let live – that's my motto. I was getting into a pattern that worked for me with my family life at home and my other life at the club house.

It seemed as though I was raising two children. Of course, one was more mentally mature then the other, but girls always are. My next lesson with my nom was to do with the birds and the bees, or in this case the nom and the Kitty. Kitten was a 21-year-old woman. She would turn up to all the Rebels bike shows. She was a cool chick. She used to work as a hooker at most of Sydney's top brothels through the week and party hard at our club house on the weekends. She would treat our club houses as her own candy store. She would turn up to our club houses and have sex with whoever she wanted and she was always treated with the same respect we showed each other. At one such show at Bringelly one weekend I introduced Kitten to John. She led him off to one of the cabins we had on the property and did her thing with him. The next time I saw Kitty was at my place. It seems as though John had a thing for her.

My first expression was anger. I had explicitly told John to never bring any woman to the house because of the little girl at home. He had various places he could have taken Kitten to but he chose to bring her to my apartment; he chose to defy my rule. I sincerely hoped he was not having any intention of passing the night with Kitten, I wasn't going to allow that. If he had brought her to meet me, he could have done that in the club or something; besides, Kitten was no stranger to me, we knew each other well. Having John bring her to the house didn't sit well with me; it was downright annoying. I felt like throwing both of them out of the house but with the last ounce of self-respect in me I exercised a little bit of restraint. Besides, no damage had been done yet. I didn't think Reese had met her yet so there was no cause for panic. I didn't want my daughter to meet Kitten; I didn't want the little girl to be influenced by this party girl. As long as Reese was kept out of all this, then everything was fine. Besides, Kitten was a good girl, she would never say or do anything inappropriate in front of Reese while she was there, and John must have really liked her a lot to have brought her here. So, at least I had to respect John's decision first; he must have a very good reason for bringing her to my house. Kitten was not just any woman; she was popular among the guys. She was a classy girl who respected herself a lot. If she and John had a good thing going, I don't think I was in any position to object.

Now let me explain how Kitty was. As long as you let her do her own thing everything was cool. She was an independent girl; she was brought up to never allow anyone dictate her life for her, no matter how important that person was. She lived in her own world where she would not have to submit to any man. I can say Kitty was the perfect picture of an independent feminist. If you tried to make her your girl and keep her from doing her thing, the claws would come out she would turn on you so fast your head would spin. She hated the idea of having to be committed to anyone; she was always all business. While in her business a lot of men out there had tried to put her under their wings, they had tried to tame her but they had all failed; Kitty would never be tamed. She was herself; if you wanted her you would have to accept her for the person she was; she would not take anything less – she would not compromise herself, her identity, for any man. She always emphasized that no man in the world could submit her and she had been staying true to that emphasis. She was no different from most bikies; you couldn't make them what they weren't. Even though Kitty really liked John, she started getting wilder and wilder the more she was caged in; only having sex with John, after a week of having to fuck old dirty men, was starting to show. So, one day while she was staying over, I thought about something interesting to do about Kitty. I was bored anyway so I needed something exciting to keep my blood flowing as usual. I went into the nom's room and told him I needed Kitty for a while; he didn't object. I got her out of bed naked and as she was about to dress up I stopped her; told her she was alright, she didn't need to get dressed, and then I walked her out of the room and into another room where Ahmed was staying. He had come over for the weekend and was sleeping in Reese's room while she was at her dad's parents' home for the weekend.

I walked Kitty into Ahmed's room and she looked at me with a smile on her face saying "Are you sure it's all right?"

"It's fine, Kitty," I assured her, smiling broadly to her.

So, she did her thing and went back to John's room when she finished. John never said anything but I think he had a better understanding that you must not try to change people. If you can't accept them for what or who they are, then it's you that has the problem. He understood, I think. He already knew the kind of girl he was dating, something like that always comes with the package.

Skirmish

A few more months would pass and the club was starting to have a few skirmishes with other clubs here and there, but nothing serious; just drive by and a few bashings if other clubs came into Rebels territory without being invited. This was mainly all out of Western Sydney. At the time the Barg wanted to expand to the East so he nommed up a few boys from Manly. One of these boys was Rick DeStoop, a 120 kg body builder who grew up in the East. I met him a few times, but he seemed a bit arrogant so I didn't really spend much time with him. I always knew people who I shouldn't associate myself with so that there would not be problems between us the fact that he was a body building didn't mean he should feel like Goliath. I can bet I would take him down in a matter of seconds. As a matter of fact, I like putting people like him in their places. Maybe someday our paths would cross again and I would be forced to deal with him. When it came to Rick and his mate getting their colours the vote was 70-30: 70% voted No and 30% Yes. So, they had to do another three months before the next vote. Being spoilt little rich boys from the East, they handed in their vests and left.

I found out later that the members who wanted them in had helped them out a fair bit with cars, drugs and bikes. Everything that you could sell and make money from was given to them on tick. It seemed that Rick was quick to take but slow in returning, so he left owing a fair bit of money to one or two members who had helped him out while he was a nom with us. But this wasn't my problem; what other members did was on them. The money wasn't for the club, so each member had to collect his own debts of course. If they had asked for help there is no doubt any other member, they asked would take it on, as if it was their own debt. Still, I was never asked for help but I knew Rick owed money and if the opportunity came up, I would act on it.

I never liked Rick, and when I started seeing him around the Cross with the Bandidos I liked him even less; he was not my kind of person. Whenever he made an appearance wherever I was, I always created as much distance between us as possible. A few times we ran into each other and just gave each other a small nod of the head just to acknowledge each other; at the point we were in, that was as much compliment as we could give each other. I didn't want to drink, smoke, snort or have any discussion with him. We had absolutely nothing in common. One night I ran into him with Sasha, the president of the Pyrmont chapter of the Bandidos. Since I had gotten my colours I wasn't spending as much time in the Cross or with other clubs, but I always had time for Sash. So, we had a few drinks together. But Rick just sat there not getting involved, and I couldn't relax with him there knowing he owed my brothers money and he still had made no effort to pay it back. I was getting really uncomfortable. It was bad enough that I didn't like the guy, he still owed a member of my club money. I wanted to hurt him, I wanted to do terrible things to him, and if I stayed any longer there, things might escalate, and I didn't want to be the one to cause problem there. So, I said I had to go meet someone and made a polite exit. The next time I would see Rick DeStoop and Sasha would be in the cellar of the Blackmarket six months later.

Over the next few weeks, I continued to deal with my club life and my home life. What I never expected was for those two to collide; I thought I was dealing with both lives well. I was dealing with an issue that I wasn't very happy about. One of my cousins who worked as a bouncer was being wooed by the Bandidos. They were inviting him to all the parties and giving him access to plenty of drugs and women, things he was not used to. He was a good kid and I felt responsible for him because I showed him this lifestyle a few years earlier. He told me he was having troubles at home when I ran into him in the Cross one night. I took him in and showed him how to make money and got him out of the business after he had a car, bike and some money to spend. But he got addicted to the fast life and when I let him go, he went straight for the Bandidos to whom I had introduced him. So, when I found out they were making him a prospect (nom) I was dirty. The last place I wanted him to belong was among the Bandidos; that was not the kind of life meant for him. if he had joined my club it would have been a lot better but it was the Bandidos that were trying to pull him in. I didn't want to imagine what he was going to become if he became one of the Bandidos. Surely, his lifespan would be cut short. He was a good kid; he wasn't cut out for the kind of violence that came with being a member of the Bandidos. These people were always having rivals and engaging in shootout with enemies. It wouldn't be long before he was taken down. It was bad enough that I was neck-deep in this kind of life, it was wrong for my cousin to follow in my footsteps.

At first, I called Sash and told him not to do it, and that my cousin was not like us. But Sash didn't really listen to me. He told me what I wanted to hear but still continued to keep my cousin with him. Over the next few weeks, a number of Bandidos met up with me to discuss my cousin, but none of them were interested in letting him go, no matter how much I tried to change their minds. I knew eventually my cousin would get sick of it and leave but I didn't want him getting too involved before that happened, or that he might get killed before he discovered that he had made the wrong choice. If he died, his death would be on me. I would not be able to forgive myself for letting that happen; but really there was nothing I could do to keep him away. My hands were figuratively tied. All I could hope for at this point was that he wouldn't get killed. There was not much more I could do other than let them know how I felt about them trying to make my cousin a member. My own club respected my wishes when I told them I didn't want my cousin in any club, and I thought that the Bandidos respected me more than that. But there was nothing more I could do. So, I let it go until I found out he was owing money to the Bandidos and one night the President, Sasha and Rick

DeStoop caught up with him and beat him barely alive. I was mad with rage. In a way, I wasn't angry about the system of the Bandidos; that was the way they did their things. What really got me upset was that Rick, the person I disliked with passion, had the mind to put his hands on my cousin. For some reason I felt he must have done the most beating; he must have beaten my cousin so hard just to spite me. I wanted to get my hands on Rick. I wanted to do all those things I had imagined doing to him over the years – but again, my hands were tied. If I attacked Rick for beating up my cousin, the Bandidos would frown on it. To them, and probably to everyone else, Rick did nothing wrong. He just did what was expected of him as a member of the Bandidos. He most probably did what he did because he knew that his club would protect him. All the same, I was blinded with rage. If I met Rick nothing would stop me from beating him as hard as he beat my cousin – that was if I didn't eventually kill him. I might have to forfeit my club membership afterward but I would know that I had finally dealt with the foul bacteria called Rick. I began to search for him.

One night I was at Bringelly after the church meeting. It was coming on to midnight by the time we finished and I got back into my car to go home. Because the phones didn't work in Bringelly, I always left my phone in the car. A few kilometres from the club house I switched it on and noticed Jane tried calling a few times. Jane never called me when I was at the club house so I knew it must have been important, so I called her back. She told me that this guy came to our flat and buzzed up to the flat we were living in. I had a security system where the person trying to get in had to be buzzed in by the occupant. There was also a video camera so you could see the person while talking to him.

Jane explained that this guy wanted to see me, and when she asked for his name, he wouldn't give it. Jane also made a point of telling me he was being very arrogant. Now for Jane to say that about someone said a lot to me because Jane got along with everyone no matter how much of an asshole they were. I got Jane to explain to me what he looked like and by the time I finished asking all my questions I was in no doubt it was Milperra, the Bandido I had met at the Cross. I wondered what the deal was between these Bandidos and me; and why had they come to my house of all places? It was a line they shouldn't cross and they had crossed it. I always let my club and business life stay away from my home, from my family. Now having Milperra behave arrogantly to my woman was not something I would just let slide. I could feel the veins on my head stand out as Jane explained her experience to me.

I was fuming and speeding faster than usual. I told Jane not to worry, but I called a few of my friends and asked them to go to my place and park out the front until I got there; I was still a long way away from home. I wished I could just fly and arrive there in a jiffy. I wished I could meet up with Milperra still around my apartment. I wished a lot of things but none of them involved any of the Bandidos leaving there safely. I explained the situation to my friends and hung up. Now before I go on any further let me explain one of the rules every MC followed back then: a member's home, family and workplace are off limits. Even if there was a war between two clubs, member's homes, family and workplaces are off limits. This was one rule I have always respected. After all those years in the Cross where there were no rules, this was a pleasant change. That was always my only worry living the life I chose. That's why I always kept my real family at arm's length. But after joining the club this issue became less of a problem, so on my way home I had to make a decision on what to do and the decision was easy. I needed to strike back fast.

I parked my car a few streets away from home and I picked up the burner. Over the years, Old Bob (the security adviser I used to go away with every weekend to learn everything I could off him) taught me a few things. In time of war, it's always good to have a vehicle close by with easy access. I would buy a cheap car from one of my friends' car yards to keep my guns in, and just in case I needed to do something like what I was about to do, or if things went to shit, I could dump and burn the car. The owner of the car yard could just say he didn't even know it was missing from the yard. So, I got into the burner, checked my gun and drove straight to the Bandidos Pyrmont club house. I didn't go home yet; I needed to do something first. In situations like this I always pride myself on my calmness; I did things a lot better with a clear head. I always allow my brain to function before my emotions take over. If I had not been thinking right, I would have driven straight home, and I would have most probably been talked out of what I was going to do by Jane, who now knew me better then I knew myself.

It was now after midnight on a Thursday night; no cars around but the lights were on in the club house, which was an old post office converted to a club house. I parked out the front and walked over to the front door, ringing the buzzer and knocking at the same time. The Beretta was down the front of my jeans with the safety off and already half-cocked. I continued to bang on the door and hit the buzzer but no one was coming to the door. I could tell someone was there because I could hear movement inside, so it was making me even angrier that they wouldn't answer me. They must have noticed me drive in and known what I had come to do. I didn't really understand why they had chosen not to answer me. Were they scared of me or something? I continued banging the door in anger and asking them to let me in or I was going to break down the door. Of course, I wasn't going to break down the door; I wasn't Rambo or something, I just had to say something, anything that would make them open the door. But still I was ignored.

At that point I was only going to let Sash – or whoever was there – know that I was not happy about Milperra going to my home. I knew I was in the right so unless it was a deliberate act, I knew they would just cop it and hopefully apologize. But the longer they ignored me the angrier I got. After what seemed to be a long enough time trying to get in, I turned around and started to go back to the burner. But I felt like I was being played so I pulled the Beretta out and fired three quick shot through the front door and got back into the car. That would send them a good message, I supposed. I wouldn't just be disrespected that way and then just walk away. Their action here had shown me that they knew exactly what was going on and they supported it. It was an indication that they didn't give a damn about the rules. Clearly the rules didn't mean anything to this bunch. If Milperra could go to my house to ask of me, then that meant that he was willing to hurt my family. For what reason exactly was he doing that? Just to show that they were not people to mess with or what. If that was their message, they had just given me a good reason to really mess with them. When you go after a man's family, what do you expect? Do you expect the man to just fold his arms and watch? Of course not, the man would do everything he could to protect his family. Before you get to his family, you will have to pass through him first. They had taken the fight to my home and I was going to fight them back really hard.

As soon as I was a few streets away I put the gun back into safety and drove back to my car. As soon as I got back to my car and switched my mobile back on, I was flooded with messages from my club. It seems that there really was someone there at the Bandidos club house, and they were calling everyone in my club they could to try and sort out this disagreement. The fact that I put three shots into their club house was never mentioned, but an apology was made and I promised I would leave it at that. But of course I had no intention of leaving it like that. I wanted to let them all know that they had messed with the wrong person. If this would mean that I would forfeit my membership in my club, then so be it. You cannot go after my family and expect that whatever else follows would be roses and daisies. The Bandidos had asked for my trouble and I was ready to give it to them hot. I have never been a chicken; even if I was against a million Bandidos I was willing to go down fighting.

Eventually it became clear that they had no intention of hurting my family. They acknowledged that Milperra had made a mistake seeking me out in my home. But the damage had already been done. After that I couldn't live in that flat with Jane and her daughter there, so I asked Jane to find a house. I told her I wanted to move into a house so I could bring my pit bull home. I had my dog at my sister's house in the West, so I thought this was a good reason why I wanted to move out of our flat. Jane started looking for a house in Bondi and the shit with Milperra was put to the side. After that the Bandidos were inviting Rebels to all their parties and my cousin was out of their club. He went back home, got married and lived the life he was meant to live. Well, considering what had happened and what might have happened, that was good news. At least my cousin was alive. I was willing to let bygones be bygones now that things were returning back to normal, but still I was not going to allow the same thing repeat itself, especially the one that involved a member of the Bandidos coming to my home. They were not as refined as the Rebels. Even though we might occasionally drink together, there was that difference between the Rebels and the Bandidos. To me, the Bandidos seemed like mere thugs who knew nothing besides living carelessly and inciting violence. They claim to be organized but in my opinion the organization was nothing to write home about. I wouldn't advise anyone I knew to join the Bandidos. They could join some other club out there, even the unknown ones, but the Bandidos were not my cup of tea, so to speak, don't get me wrong there were a lot of members in their club that I respected, but many of them were just living of the reputation from the Milperra massacre.

War

In the next few weeks while Jane was looking for a new place, the club houses in the West were going off. We were at the verge of all out war with a few other clubs: one major club and a few smaller one trying to get a reputation by taking on the Rebels. One of these smaller clubs – let's call them the Grave Robbers – in Newcastle did something that even impressed me. What they did was one of the most daring things ever done, and when I heard about it I thought to myself these guys must all be ex-military with balls the size of cannon balls – or they were all on acid and didn't know what they were doing. Either way they had my respect. People hardly gained my respect because I had seen a lot of shit in my days, but these Grave Robbers did things I never thought anyone would have the balls to attempt.

So, this is what they did. Our boys moved into a suburb in Newcastle, set up a chapter and started to get to know the locals. This was a standard practice when you move into a new area. It was also the reason why we were having so many skirmishes with other clubs all over; this is what happens when you expand, and the Rebels were expanding at a fast pace. One weekend, as the Newcastle chapter was setting up for a party where the locals would be invited, five members of the Grave Robbers ran in on the Newcastle chapter of the Rebels. There were four Rebels and two noms there setting up, but they were caught by surprise. The Grave Robbers had chains and bats, and one had a shot gun. Our boys never had a chance. They fought back but will and guts were no match for surprise and weapons. It was a full-blown attack. They used all the weapons they had at their disposal. Even though they attacked only a few of us, they carried out the attack as if they had come to fight the entire club. They wouldn't have prepared better if their mission was to assassinate the President of a country. We Rebels had strong hearts; we were trained to fight hard no matter the situation. We hardly launch any attack at any club, but whenever we were attacked, we always held our own. But this particular attack was a no show for our boys.

Three Rebels went to hospital with gunshot wounds to the knees and one with a cracked skull. It was a miracle that the one with the cracked skull wasn't dead. Apparently, the Grave Robbers had not come to kill them, they had only come to show their strength, to let us know that they might be inferior but they should not be underestimated. And with that stunt they pulled with our guys, they sure had our attention – indeed they had my attention. I was curious about them; I wanted to know their way. Who had given them the confidence to attack one of our own? What were they hoping to achieve with that attack? Were they trying to send us a kind of message? A lot of questions were roaming in my head; and there was no doubt that I was highly impressed by the way they carried out the attack; it was coordinated and clean. The other boys patched themselves up but they would never be the same. In a way, I was glad that I was not in the wrong place at the wrong time. Those boys had not come to play poker with us. They had just showed us that they meant some serious business, that they were ready for war – in fact, they wanted the war, and that was why they brought it to us. It was clear what they wanted; they were ambitious and they wanted to use us to make names for themselves. As impressive as I thought they were, I couldn't but agree that they were stupid. They had chosen the wrong club to make themselves relevant. The Grave Robbers used a small pellet in the shot gun, something like bird shot, so it wasn't as bad as first thought. It seems as though they just wanted to send a message, but when they took three sets of colours off our boys then there was only one way we could react. Putting it simply it's like someone taking your shoes and then saying, "What are you going to do about it?" You only have two options, right? You put your head down and walk home barefooted or you fight back. That was the kind of audacity they displayed to us. They took the colours off the boys to let us know that they were ready for whatever consequence that came with it. And of course, the Rebels were not scared little boys that would walk home barefoot crying. We would punch the takers in the mouth and get back our shoes, and the Grave Robbers expected nothing less. There wasn't going to be any fun if we cowered home like puppies with their tails between their legs – that was not who we were anyway. I guess that was the reason they attacked our boys.

Well with Rebels there is only one option: fight back until there is full and utter annihilation. But first you must get the colours back undamaged. After the raid on our club house by the Grave Robbers we were told to put into place the procedure we had for times of war. First, we made sure our families were safe, then we stopped all weekend party nights, and finally: no more riding or wearing anything that identifies you as a member of the Rebels. Basically, we went underground. Actually, to most people it would seem like a cowardly move, but it was far from that. We had learned that it was better to fight smart than to fight hard. By trying to strike back at our enemies, we didn't want more casualties on our parts, most especially on our families. So, we all had the responsibility of making sure that we took our family members to places where no rival club could get to them. Just like the Bandidos, some clubs didn't give a damn about the rules that states that no family must be involved. In fact, some clubs now specialize in intimidating families of rival club members; they figured that the best way to hurt enemies was if their families were hurt. I couldn't imagine anything bad happening to Jane and her daughter just because I had chosen to become a Rebel. I didn't sign up for that kind of life, so I must do everything I could to protect them well. If they were safely hidden away, I could concentrate on the things that need to be done. I could face my enemies without worrying about the safety of my family.

As the days went by after the raid, the Grave Robbers started to realize what the implications of their actions could be. So they started to try and make contact with us so they could broker some sort of agreement. But our club was not going to have any talks with the Grave Robbers until the colours were returned. So a deal was set to give the three sets of colours back. Bringelly had a meeting with representatives from each chapter in NSW. Bear and I were there for the city chapter. The situation was explained, and volunteers were asked for. Every member put their hands up, but the decision was already made before the meeting that Bear and I would go to Newcastle to meet with the Grave Robbers to get our colours back. The show of hands was just so no one felt left out.

This meeting with the Grave Robbers had been carefully discussed and strategized by the senior members of the club and it was decided that the Grave Robbers would most likely give the colours back. But there was also a good chance they would go kamikaze on us and put a bullet in our heads declaring all-out war. For me it was a no-brainer, and with my knowledge of warfare strategies so gratefully passed on to me by old Bob, I had the best chance of working out if it was a setup. And I already had my contingency plan in place. I wouldn't trust the Grave Robbers with my life. After the stunts they pulled against our boys before taking their colours, I knew they shouldn't be trusted. I was not going to stand in their presence without having a personal plan of my own. We could be walking into an ambush. This was not the first time that a peace deal had turned into a slaughter. They could just be luring us into their net and when we were comfortable, smother us all. I wouldn't put anything past this club.

On a bright sunny day in 1997, Bear and I jumped into the beast and headed for Newcastle. The tension was thick from the moment we got into the beast; not one word was spoken all the way there. I was thinking of everything that could happen, and the fact that our colours were in enemy hands was like fuel to my determination. I was set to either get our colours back or go out with a bang. I was sure that was the same thing Bear was thinking. I felt a little bit of relief knowing that Bear was with me. Even without saying it we knew we had each other's backs. There was no way we would go down without taking a considerable number of them down with us. This might be the last trip I could be making in my life. I was a man who would not back out from a fight, even if the fight might seem to be an already lost one.

It was agreed by both sides there would be no guns, and when a bikie gives his word you can bet on it "usually". But I wasn't taking anyone's word. I was putting my life on the line and if things went belly up, I was going to make sure I at least did some damage. I didn't bring a gun because, after all, one of my brothers gave their word we wouldn't be armed. So, I honoured that, but I wasn't going into a situation where there was a good chance, I would get a bullet in the head. So, in light of not having any weapons, I brought a US issue hand grenade. It was the size of a handball (just a bit smaller than a tennis ball) and it had a 3-second fuse on it so when you pull the pin you have three seconds from the time your hand releases the trigger mechanism, which was a bar running alongside of the contour of the grenade. As soon as you threw it the trigger mechanism would fly off and in three seconds "BANG". My plan was to pull the pin and have it wedged between my knee and the door panel. If I got shot, there was no way out: my knee would go limp and three seconds later whoever was near me and the car would get some shrapnel damage, depending on where they were. It was a dangerous and suicidal plan. A lot of things could go wrong. What if nobody wanted to shoot me but for some reason my knees shifted from their position? I might just kill myself and a couple of other people for no good reason. I decided that I was going to be as careful as possible.

I didn't tell Bear about it because I wasn't sure how he would react. I had done this many times before when making drug deals with new people, so I decided it was best he didn't know. The trip to Newcastle was quick. It only took me half the time it would normally take thanks to a new toy I just had fitted to the beast a few weeks before. It was a radar detector from the States; it was sent to me by a friend saying it was undetectable to the equipment Australia was using at the time. So, I put it through its paces. It only went off once, and I had plenty of time to slow down. I thought it was playing up, but it had picked up the cop's radar from a long way away. That was why I thought it was broken, because it kept on indicating way before any other detector. But when I finally saw the cop car, I knew it was good. This was indeed what I needed for myself, and it had come in handy at the right moment. I could always travel at any speed I wanted without having to get tickets from the cops. It was an incredible piece of equipment.

Finally, we got to Newcastle two hours early. We headed for one of our member's tattoo shops so we could get briefed properly on everything about these Grave Robbers and exactly how everything went down on that night they got raided by them. We had already heard the story but it's always good to hear from the people that were there. So, as we waited for the phone call from the

Grave Robbers to tell us where they wanted us to meet for the handover, we got a pretty good idea of who these guys were. It seemed like they were just some young outlaws trying to make a name for themselves. That worried me, but when I heard that their President was a much older man, I felt a bit better. The Newcastle boys knew we didn't have any guns on us and offered some, but Bear said "NO" as I knew he would. He was willing to hold up the end of our deal; I was sure he wouldn't have allowed me to go with him if I had accepted the guns. Nothing changed what I had already known about Bear; he was ready to go to the last mile with me but he was not going to mess up the negotiation by carrying a firearm. We had assured them that we wouldn't be coming armed; Bear was always a man of his words, and I didn't fault him with that. In fact, I admired him for choosing to be honest in the dealings. This conviction was not made because the senior members of the Rebels had told us not to carry weapons, Bear simply believed that things could be done amicably. It was an extension of trust, a form of olive branch. However, if things went sour as I suspected they might, Bear would fight till his last breath. He was one of the bravest sons of bitches I've ever known.

Finally, the call came in. Bear was doing all the communication with them. They wanted us to go and park in front of the courthouse. I thought at first this was good; it's a busy area with plenty of people and cops. That last part of the equation I wasn't too happy about but still, if the handover was going to be done there, then there was no chance of an assassination attempt. So, when we got there and parked right in front of the courthouse, I didn't even bother to get the grenade out of its secret hiding place in the door trim. We sat there for about 10 minutes. At this point, I was relaxed. I didn't expect that they would pull anything funny on us in this open area. Perhaps they had chosen this place because they didn't trust that we would hold up our own end of the deal either. Perhaps they believed we came with weapons and they were not ready to take any chance. Well, they were slightly right. Whatever the case might be, the ball was still in their court. I still couldn't help but feel like we were sitting duck out there. A sniper might be stationed in one of the tall buildings and simply take us out as soon as given the order. If that was the case it would mean that the Grave Robbers had won again; I would die without having to take any enemy along with me. All my contingency plans would go to shit. But I was most probably just being paranoid; none of all the stuff I had imagined would ever happen. The Grave Robbers were as much willing to get over the tension just as we were.

During this time, Bear and I were on full alert. We studied every person to go by and everyone else in eye view. I spotted two guys that could have been bikies sussing us out, one from across the road and the other at a bus stop. After ten minutes Bear got another call. This time they wanted us to go to a McDonald's close by. This was also a busy area and it was looking more and more likely that they were more worried about us shooting them at the handover. So, the change of locations was to see if we had others there with us. This was good. It looked like they really did want to give back the colours. And the obvious was clear – they were scared of us, scared of what we were going to do. I wasn't sure if they were out of the woods even after they handed over the colours. They had drawn the first blood, there should be hell to pay. If I were the leader of the Rebels, I knew exactly how I was going to retaliate; I would strategically wipe them off the face of the earth, even if it was going to take me years to achieve. But it seemed like the Rebels were up for a truce with the Grave Robbers. A group of men cannot just attack you in your territory and you will sit down and fold your hands. They had disrespected us, and I expected that there would be a form of payback. Well, I was willing to see how things were going to unfold.

After another ten minutes at McDonald's, Bear got another call. This time they wanted us to go to a street about four blocks away. Okay, this was beginning to get annoying. I was starting to feel like the guys were turning us to errand boys that would just be running around the neighbourhoods; this was getting me uncomfortable, and of course upset. Why couldn't they just hand over the colours and get things over with? One thing was to be extremely careful; another thing was to just be annoying. As I turned into the street, I noticed there was a car behind us with two guys in it (Grave Robbers). Finally, we could see that they were with us. I couldn't tell whether they had been following us right from the start or not, but at least the handover was going to happen. The street they chose for the actual handover was very quiet and isolated so as soon as I pulled over, the other car behind me also pulled over; well, that was expected. I wasn't sure if they knew that I had spotted them, but it didn't matter anyway. Whatever was going to happen here, I was ready – I was prepared. I then quickly put it in park and got the grenade out. I pulled the pin and wedged it between my right knee and the door trim. I also lowered my window and rested my right elbow on the widow showing my right hand was empty apart from the little steel ring with a split pin hanging off it. My other hand was on the steering wheel. I did this so I didn't spook them. Bear also put his window down and rested his left elbow on it. Still, he hadn't noticed the grenade I had brought with us. I was sure he would freak out if he knew what I intended to do. I wasn't afraid to die; it was just sad that when I would be blown to smithereens with my enemies, Bear would be a casualty too. I didn't think he planned to die to a bomb explosion. But he would agree that it was better to die with a bang than to just get killed like a stray dog. I always hoped people would tell interesting stories whenever they explained how I died to other people. Bear and I would be considered martyrs by the Rebels; perhaps our deaths would make them grow stronger and more important among other clubs. Well, we were strong and important anyway. If we were not relevant, the Grave Robbers would not have attacked us in the first place; they wouldn't have had the guts to use us to make names for themselves in this world. I hoped that they got to learn that they had just stuck their collective hands into a hornet's nest – I'd like to know that whether I was alive or dead.

As we parked, another car came out of the side street in the opposite direction from where we came from, stopping right in front of us nose to nose. The two in that car stayed in their car; the other two behind us got out and went straight to Bear's side. At point I remember thinking if something happened now I wouldn't be able to do as much damage as I thought. I was anticipating there would be a few on my side as well but only two got out. Bear got out to get our colours from the car behind us. I watched him pick up a bag, look inside and then go straight to my boot indicating to me to open it. This wasn't good. I thought if the positions were reversed, I would be prepared for someone to open fire from the boot when we opened it. But it looks like they didn't think of that. They were just happy to get rid of the colours they took off our boys. It seemed like they kept their end of the deal too – that was a sign of good faith. If we had not kept up ours, we would have ambushed them and just killed these people – and I didn't think that would be a terrible idea after all. But then again, that action would make us lose face in the general public; no club or organization would trust us or want to have anything to do with us. Seeming untrustworthy would not be good on our image. Perhaps it was because of this image that the senior members of the Rebel agreed that it was fine to get back the colours without putting up any fight. If not for that, we might have annihilated the entire Grave Robbers club. But I knew that these leaders always had clandestine meetings where they discussed how to relate with one another.

As soon as Bear was handed the colours they jumped back into their cars and took off. It went well after all. I had thought it was going to end in disaster. As Bear was putting the colours in the boot, I slowly put the pin back in and hid the grenade back in its slot. Bear got back in and we took off, relieved it went well. After making all the calls to let everyone know there were no issues, I put the

music on and cruised back to Bringelly. The drive back
was much more relaxing than the drive up. The feeling
you get is like when you get on a roller coaster or bungee
jump; the feeling you get after doing something like that is
the feeling I had, a sense of accomplishment and relief that
the worst is over. Now I would go home and appreciate
my time with family and friends. I dropped Bear off at
Bringelly with the colours and I headed back to Bondi.
Not one person was hurt "that day".

Family Life

The next few weeks were pretty much uneventful. Jane
found a new place to move into in Bondi and I had my
reporting conditions changed so I didn't have to drive to
Glebe every day. Now I just had to report two times a
week at Bondi cop shop. I remember after moving into
the house with Jane, Reese and my dog, I started to think
this was much better than the time before when I tried
doing the family thing. I wasn't trying to be someone I
wasn't this time. This time around, John didn't move in
with us. It was a relief that he didn't choose to join us in
this new apartment. As a matter of fact, I think he wanted
to live with his girlfriend, Kitty – and who am I to stand
in the way of love? But if you want my honest opinion,
I didn't think Kitty and John's relationship was going to
last. Knowing that your girlfriend has sex with various
guys every night will eventually be too much for you to
bear. One day you will put your feet down and say No.
Then that's when the problems will start. Like I already
said, Kitty wasn't a girl who appreciated people telling her
what to do or what they expected of her. Eventually, both

would find out that they were not made for each other and they would part ways. Even if that was not the case, even if John continued to remain fine that his girl was always sleeping around with men for money, Kitty will sooner or later ruin their relationship. I don't see her as a girl that fancied settling down. Besides the fact that she slept with men for money, I think it was also her hobby. She would sleep with any man she fancied without any charges. She was not a one-man kind of girl. I didn't understand what John must have told her to make her agree to be his girlfriend – for, damn, that girl was not a one-man girl. You don't even have to look good or be rich to be able to get Kitty. Just be bold and have the right words in your mouth and she would be riding the life out of you. My experience with her was that she was a professional; perhaps that was why John wanted her so much – because she was a great woman in bed. Most people were surprised to discover that John and Kitty were going out. Some of them had laughed hard at the imagination of the two getting married. I think even John was aware of all the sniggers behind his back, but he didn't seem to care. Kitty was the woman he wanted and he went for her; anyone who had a dissenting opinion could go to hell and stay there. He was with Kitty and there was nothing anyone could do about it.

I later realised that John moved into the new club house we opened in Redfern because the house we moved to only had two bedrooms, one for Jane and me and the other for Reese. I was trying to make it as stable a family unit as possible, but the truth be told, the only normal person in our family unit was Jane's daughter. Even though she was only eight years old she had more sense than me and Jane put together. I remember our family walks in Bondi. We would walk around the neighbourhood as a normal family, but we weren't. I would put on my favourite T-shirt, put the leash on my dog and walk to the cop shop to report with Jane and Reese. Imagine this bikie, a stripper and a very mentally mature eight-year-old girl walking a Pit-bull. I would go into the cop station and wait at the front desk for service while Jane and Reese along with the dog waited for me outside. It was an incredible thing to happen to me. I considered myself the luckiest person in the world. I'm not saying Jane wasn't smart – hell, she was way smarter than me, but Reese was still smarter than the two of us put together. Sometimes it felt like we were the children and Reese was the parent. We learnt a lot of morality from that little girl. That was why I didn't want anyone tainting her innocence. That was why I strictly told John never to bring any of his whores to the house whenever Reese was around. I always kept her protected from the cruel world as possible. But no matter how much I tried to protect her, sooner or later she was going to grow up and make her own choice in life. What if she decided that she wanted to follow in her mother's footsteps? Well, I wouldn't really bat an eye if she decided that she wanted to work an honest job in a restaurant; but I would probably die of heart attack if she decided that she wanted to be a stripper, or a model. I wanted a much better profession for Reese. She could work in the medical field, she could be a lawyer, she could be the CEO of a Fortune 500 company. There were a lot of other professions she could choose from.

Now you might think ok that's not very interesting, but here is where my Rebel personality makes it a bit more interesting. You see a few months ago when Reese's dad came to pick her up for the weekend (oh yes, he didn't die or something), he brought me a few T-shirts that he thought I might like, and he was right. They were novelty T-shirts, and my favourite was the one I would wear every time I went to report at Bondi cop shop. It was a white T-shirt with the Calvin Klein logo on it in big black letters: "CK". But when you look closely at the small writing beside the C and the K, it didn't say Calvin or Klein, it said Cop Killer. I would walk out of that cop shop every time with the biggest smile on my face. Reporting was never so much fun. It was not like I had killed any cop before; well, I could say the same for the person who gave me the shirt – I don't really know. But it was good wearing that shirt around. Maybe someday it was going to get me in trouble when any passing cop took a good look at it and saw the spellings; but for now, it was one of my most favourite shirts. Truthfully, a lot of these cops deserved to be killed, many of them were corrupt officers, and if anyone could step up to kill them, I would admire the person. The world would be a better place if there were no more corrupt police officers making life unbearable for both the innocent and the guilty. Do you know the number of innocent people who have been sent to jail for crimes they didn't commit? A lot! And this was because of the abuse of power by these corrupt cops.

But in reality, my court case for the drug charges was getting closer and I had Jane and Reese to think about now. So, I started spending more and more time with the accountant to try and set this company up so Jane and Reese didn't have to worry about making ends meet while I was gone. There was no doubt I was going to jail, and that didn't worry me. What worried me was leaving Jane and Reese behind. So, I worked on the company. I sold the beast and leased a Porsche, and I even sold my Harley after the National run. Prison was built to punish people like me, it was only a matter of time before I joined them. And I knew that I would not be there indefinitely; I didn't think I had committed enough crime to warrant a life sentence. However, I might become an old man by the time I was released from prison. This was what I actually dread. I didn't want to waste my prime away in prison always looking behind me for someone who might just want to shank me for the hell of it.

The Rebels broke off after that for a few months so we could spend time with the family. At the end of the year, we always had two months where there were no compulsory meetings or runs. This way we could go away with the family. So, after the last run for the year, I sold the bike, thinking I would be in jail before the next run, and in a way I was right. It's just that I would not be in jail for drug charges; I would be there for triple murder and one attempted murder. If someone had told me that this was what would happen to me, I would have done two things to the person: it was either one, pat him on the shoulder and laugh hard, or I just punch him in the face for coming up with such ridiculous prophecy – my reaction would depend on my mood at the time. The point was that I would never have believed that I would be charged for killing a dog let alone triple murders; it just didn't make any sense to me.

Well, that was still a few months away. Until then life was good. Jane and I would spend most days with the accountant and his wife, and every now and then John would pop in with a new girl. Whenever he appeared with those new chicks, I always wondered if he was still with Kitty. Was it their agreement that they could sleep with whoever they wanted? Well, that would be the most sensible thing, considering their situation. Open relationship could very well work for them. In fact, they could even get married and continue sleeping with other people. But then again, knowing Kitty's temperament, it was hard to imagine that she would agree with something like this. Maybe their relationship was over. I didn't want to believe that I had been correct all along; I didn't want to agree that John had finally broken and called it quits with the woman he claimed he liked so much. I wanted to ask him but thought better of it. Whatever he chose to do with his romantic life was none of my business. As a matter of fact, I had my own life to think about; I couldn't go meddling into other people's affairs. I was more than that; I was not a person who delights in cheap gossips and stuff. John was a really good-looking guy who could get as many women as he wanted; he could get even ladies a lot hotter than Kitty; it was just interesting that he had to choose to start a relationship with a very popular girl. Nothing could come out of that kind of relationship except some serious heartbreak. Anyway, every pot has its own cover. I was the cover of Jane' pot – perhaps John was the cover of Kitty's pot too.

One of those times, John brought this girl over that I knew from the Cross one year earlier. Her name was Angie and she was a piece of work, and I don't mean that in a good way. She was one of these girls who loved causing dramas. She would attach herself to an Alpha male and use him for her own deeds. I first met her in the strip clubs on the main street. She had just come over from New Zealand and she was stripping on the circuit. Fatty's right-hand man introduced her to me and I didn't think twice about her until next time I saw her at Dancers. It seems as though she ate up Fatty's right-hand man on the main circuit and was using him as her own personal servant. And she was moving into the surrounding strip clubs to cause her mayhem there too, turning doormen against doormen. I remember going to Dancers one night and the girls I was very close with, complaining that this new girl was causing trouble, and money was going missing from girls' handbags. Angie was the number one suspect, but she had her claws into the owner. But I knew when girls like that get their claws in there is only one solution. I started to wonder whether John had a knack for attracting the wrong girls. First it was Kitty, and now Angie. Compared to the troubles that always followed Angie around, Kitty was an angel. I could accept Kitty, but Angie was never up to any good. She had a terrible track record among people. I knew her intention; she wanted to use John just as she had been using other men in her life. Well, I was not going to allow that to happen. This time around I was going to save John from this particular wrong choice. Angie was a gold-digger, but John was probably not seeing that. He had a knack for falling for the really terrible ones. I knew if I told John about how bad Angie was for him, he would not do anything about it; that was even if he believed me in the first place. From past experience, I had known that John wasn't one to take any advice. He only saw things in one dimension. I guess that was why a lot of ladies were taking advantage of him. But John was my boy; I was not going to sit around and watch any girl squeeze him dry, especially someone like Angie. I was sure she had been using John as a personal bodyguard; and when she got tired of him, she would dispose of him in an instant and move on to the next interesting man on the block. Angie wasn't my favourite kind of person at all, and I would not allow her to make my boy useless like she had been making other men around the clubs.

I pulled Angie to the side and told her it was time she moved on. I was very nice about it, but she also understood I wasn't asking her; and she must have heard stuff about me. I guess she just didn't want to be in any trouble with me. I made her know that I understood the kind of game she was playing, and I wouldn't allow her to play that game on someone important to me. Well, I put it to her real good and I was sure my words got to her. Perhaps also knowing that I was a Rebel made her back off real fast. She knew I could do some real damage to her. It wasn't like I was going to physically hurt her or anything, but I had the power to end her career; I could let people know that she was bad news. In fact, I could do so much damage that she would not find anyone else to use. I suppose that one thing she really dreaded was being useless; not having any man to depend on her, or to care for her. She ended up moving on and I hadn't seen her until then; indeed, good riddance. Someone like Angie should not move close to any of my family members.

While I was still talking to Angie, John walked in and before he could say anything, I said "Hello Angie." This didn't really surprise John; he knew she was a stripper so it made sense that I or Jane would know her. No eyebrows were raised. I'm not sure that he would even have minded if I had been trying to get into Angie's pants. John was just as cool as that; he wasn't a man to hoard his women, especially when he knew that they were in the sex business – sure, he knew things like that always came with the territory. That was why he was able to be with Kitty for so long – and Kitty was a lot more fun than Angie. Besides, Angie wasn't my kind of girl. I wouldn't sleep with her if she was the last woman in the world. It wasn't like she wasn't beautiful or something. As a matter of fact, John always went out with some of the hottest women around. Angie was stunning but her personality has killed whatever lust there would be, if there was going to be any. I couldn't understand how she could use so many men easily. She had a very hot body; and I could tell that most men would find her sexuality appealing, even though she might be faking the seduction just to make them do whatever she wanted. She was a chameleon, and from knowing the kind of person Angie was, I kind of respected Kitty more. At least Kitty was true to herself; she never claimed to be who she was not. This Angie, on the other hand, was a great pretender, and I easily saw through her subterfuge.

So, he came in, sat down, and filled me in on what he'd been up to since we broke off for the holidays. He was still living in the club house because it was so close to his work at the Blackmarket. It also seemed as though Angie was living with him at the club house. I told John it's ok if he wanted to live there, but we couldn't have girls or other people living there, and in my own mind I was thinking especially of this girl. But I didn't tell him about her past; I just told him to watch out for her. Like I said, John didn't like being told what to do, so I didn't try to impose my thoughts on him. I knew he would eventually work it out himself; if the girl didn't leave, he would realise that she wasn't the right person for him sooner or later. Then a few weeks later he did, he saw her for the clout that she was. Their relationship ended of course, and she left him, but not without her leaving her mark behind. As a result, John also had to bar her from coming into the Blackmarket. She knew John enough to not dare him. She knew that John was capable of making her 'disappear' and being the kind of girl she was, no one would really miss her. Men liked her voluptuous body of course, but there were hundreds of other girls with rocking body. It would take no time before they forgot about her and move on to the next hot cake. She might have been able to use John in her own way, but she knew that she mustn't get him upset. And since John had known the kind of person she was, there was no charm she would be able to use on him that would work anymore. So, she never showed herself at the Blackmarket anymore. I was sure she had carried her deception to another location, where people had not yet known her for the user she was. Women like that could not stop doing what they do; that was what made them relevant and when you take that from them, they become depressed. In a way, I wished her best of luck with her trade. I had nothing against her of course, I just didn't want her hurting the people I cared about.

Two weeks before the murders, the accountant asked me if I could show him how to use a handgun. He had a hobby farm just outside of Canberra, so he invited me and Jane there for the weekend, and at the same time I could bring some of my guns with me. Jane and the accountant's wife were all for it, so we packed the cars up one weekend, dropped Reese at her grandparents, and headed for the accountant's property. Jane and I drove in my Silver 928 Porsche that I was leasing, and the accountant in one of his rentals. As soon as we got there, the girls prepared the rooms and made something to eat while the accountant and I walked around the farm.

I had my Beretta with me, so I went through a few things with the accountant to do with gun safety before handing him the gun. He had fired a rifle before but never a handgun, so after giving him a few pointers we set up a target and went through about 50 rounds before heading back to the house for lunch. It was a normal setting, two couples talking and having lunch together outside on the patio of a serene setting. The only difference with this picture was the 9mm Smith & Wesson with the silver finish, the 9mm Beretta gun in metal black and the Ruger 10/22 submachine gun with a full barrel silencer with a laser pointer on it sitting on the table beside the soft drinks.

After lunch we all went back to where the accountant and I set up the target and I showed the girls how to fire the guns. I must admit I was a bit worried because there were three weapons there and I had to make sure everyone was safe using them. That was why I only let them fire each gun one at a time, while the others posed with empty weapons for the camera. As soon as everyone had enough of the smell of gun powder and lead, we went back to the farmhouse where the girls did their thing, and the accountant and I discussed the company we had set up while I was cleaning all the guns.

We were only three weeks away from signing all the papers and opening up the office we had set up in Bondi. The computers were in, all the phone lines and staff had already been hired, all we had to do was sign the government contracts and receive the funding. I couldn't believe how easy this was. All my life I thought the outlaw life was how easy money was made, but the real criminals were the white-collar workers in the government. It was incredibly exciting to know that I could steal money in the face of the police, and nothing could be done to me. It was like the banks that would always steal your money but would back their acts up with some mumbo-jumbo that no one would be able to sue them. I was feeling excited. It was sad that this would only go on for a short time. Soon, I would be facing my trials and I would be going to jail. But with the little time I had left I was willing to clear as many transactions as I could before the day finally arrived. At least I was going to leave something tangible for Jane and Reese. An idea occurred to me to bring in Jane into this transaction. That way, even when I was away in jail, Jane could continue the flow. It would be cool. But I didn't know how I was going to inform the accountant about that; he might find it inappropriate. I guessed it was not yet the time to pitch in that kind of idea. When the time was right, I would discuss with the man; I might even offer to cut him a certain percentage if he were going to let Jane in. If it worked out as I wanted, I might just be coming home to great wealth when I got out of jail. Okay, let me not get ahead of myself.

The weekend was great and very relaxing for me, especially after all those months of skirmishes with other clubs. It seemed like it was all over now, and I didn't have to be "ON" all the time. As soon as we got back home, I put all the guns back in the burner a few streets away, and Jane and I drove to her in-laws to pick up Reese. Reese's grandparents were very nice people; they didn't mind the fact that I was not really the father of their granddaughter. They treated me with the same respect and courtesy they would give their son. They actually considered me as a part of the family, and I was indeed grateful for that. It was nice to know that law-abiding folks considered me worthy of being among them. I never really cared about what people thought about me anyway, but it felt nice knowing that people thought nicely of you. I swore that I would not do anything that would jeopardize the respect they had for me – and to me, they could never go wrong. I had never met nicer couples than these grandparents. I guess that's why even Reese loved spending time with them so much. She was always excited whenever she was being told that she was going to visit them. Reese was a good judge of characters; it didn't matter to her that they were her grandparents, if she had thought that they were not nice she would have made the fact very obvious.

The next week was pretty much normal. Jane had changed her hours at the restaurant she was working at, so I was taking Reese to school every day and picking her up. I was really enjoying this setup, but my court case was getting closer and I knew I would have to go away for a while soon. So, I didn't allow myself to enjoy it too much. I didn't know how Reese was going to take it if she discovered that I would be going away for a long time. Having to leave her would be really painful, not only for her but also for me. Over the years, Reese and I had developed a special kind of bond. She actually saw me as a father figure, which was more than I could ask for.

The week passed, and we dropped Reese off at her dad's place again and Jane and I had plans to spend the weekend with Harry and his girlfriend. It started at Harry's place, which was also in Bondi. Ever since I gave him the money to set up his own tattoo shop in the City, he found a place close by, so he didn't have to travel to the West every day. And it was good having Harry around; he was a good guy to be with. With Harry, there was no dull moment. He had access to a lot of assorted jokes, and I thought he would make a pretty great comedian, and he was a very good tattoo artist. His girlfriend too was a very nice lady. She and Jane got along pretty well. Jane always chose her friends carefully; even when she used to be a stripper, she was not one to mix herself with just any person. She was classy with the kinds of people she associated herself with. Even though she was a hooker, she had grace; she was not a woman without brains. As a matter of fact, Jane was the only stripper I knew who had something really worthwhile in her head. And having her get along with Harry's girlfriend meant that Harry had picked up the right girl. At first, I had thought Jane was only faking being nice with Harry's girlfriend; but then again, I never knew Jane to fake anything (well, perhaps except during her stripping days). She was always a straight arrow. She never hid her feelings or what she thought about people; she always said it as she felt it. I guess that was one thing Reese picked from her. And so, having her go along with Harry's girlfriend warmed my belly. If she didn't like her, she would have openly said it and that would have ruined our time with Harry. In fact, Jane confessed that she and the girl might just be good friends. That would be incredible; Jane never really had any friends. She was always keeping to herself and minding her business, even at work she had no serious companion; they were all just acquaintances. It would be very nice knowing her friend for once. That could even bring Harry and me closer; but unfortunately, I would be going to jail soon. Maybe a friend was what she needed, someone who could keep her mind off me. I'd rather she had a female friend. Of course, I wanted Jane to be happy.

I would be going away soon and I didn't need any headaches or loose ends, once in jail I knew that I would have to cut myself out from Jane's life and concentrate on my life inside, you can't live in one world and have your mind in another, it just doesn't work, I knew once I was in jail I would have to put all my effort into that life without the worry of how my loved ones are on the outside.

4

HELLFIRE

It's Friday night the 7th of November 1997. Jane, I, Harry and his girlfriend, and Neville and another girl were all at Harry's place drinking, smoking, popping ecstasy, and snorting speed and coke. I of course, didn't have any coke; since getting busted in 1996 for drugs. I still hadn't touched it after getting out on bail, after all the shit I had gotten myself into because of it there was no way I would make the same mistake again.

I have always prided myself in the past by the way I have always reacted after making a mistake. I make a conscious decision never to make that mistake again, and this decision has served me well over the years. So, the party went on all night and into the next day. Jane and I went home a few times to shower and change but we kept ending up back at Harrys place. It was now Saturday night and all the girls wanted to go out dancing, so they got changed again. We all took some more ecstasy and headed towards the Blackmarket (Hellfire) at about 12am, Sunday 9th of November 1997.

I had stopped drinking hours before, so I drove my Porche there, it was me and Jane in the front seat, Neville and his girl in the back seat, Harry and his girlfriend were driven there by another couple that had joined us earlier that night. As soon as we got there, I noticed John wasn't on the door yet. I found out he was doing the day shift according to the other bouncers, and they didn't expect him there until 4am or 5am that morning. So, after saying hello to everyone I knew them working on the door and the girls taking the entrance fee in the foyer. I walked to my usual space to the left past the foyer in the corner next to the first bar. The girls went straight to the front dance floor, this was the first of three dance floors there. This one was on the right as you walk in, just past the cloak room. I could see the girls from my spot at the bar on the left. As the night went on, we drank and laughed with many people that we knew, it was a great night with not a worry in the world. Later on, Neville and his girl went back to the West with a friend of ours who lived there. Harry and his girl also left, going back to their place. It was just me and Jane left behind, still not ready to call it a night yet. We had run into another couple there that I knew. Dominic was a car dealer, and his wife was a beautician. They had been there all night and weren't ready to call it a night yet either, so, me and Dom sat at the bar catching up, and the girls did their thing on the dance floor. It was now about 4:30am Sunday morning, John just came in for work. He was working on the door for the Blackmarket day club, called Hellfire, his shift started about 6am. Once all the other night clubs around the City shut their doors, that was when the club would get really busy. I spoke to John for a while just to catch up, but after a while, me, Jane and Dom and his wife decided to go to our house in Bondi for breakfast. We didn't want to be in the club when all the other patriates from other night clubs started flooding the place, after all, we had been going for a while now and we were starting to wind down, so it was decided, Dom and his wife follow me and Jane back to our place in their car. Once we got back home, Jane put on the music video channel on Foxtel and started making us breakfast.

I remember it well, it was to be my last cooked meal in our Bondi home, toasted focaccia bread with diced tomato, onion, avocado, prinked with herbs, salt and pepper. As we ate there, talking with the music on in the back ground, eating our breakfast and drinking coffee, my phone rang. I got up to take the call and it was John on the other end. I asked him if everything was ok. A few hours had passed since we left the Blackmarket and John was already a few hours into his shift.

It was now 7:30am the 9th of November 1997, I am at home with Jane entertaining another couple. I am on the phone talking to John, he tells me that Sasha the President of the Pyrmont Chapter of the Bandidos is at the Blackmarket with around 14 other members of his club. He goes on to tell me that no one was wearing colours but they did have club jumpers and t-shirts identifying them as Bandidos. Now this was the first red flag. You see there has always been an agreement between the bike clubs that we would never go to a night club where other members from other bike clubs worked in numbers, it just didn't look good and it was bad for business. So, I started asking

John questions; how long have they been there? Were there any girls with them? That last question was to give me an idea whether they were there for trouble or just carrying on partying from the night before. John went on to tell me that there were 3 girls with them and the one that walked in with Mick K was Angie, red flag No2. This was very significant because Mick K was the National President of the Bandidos, a very powerful and well-respected member of the Bandidos; the fact that he walked in with Angie didn't really mean much to me. I knew her personality and assumed she didn't tell the Bandidos she was barred, this was how she always manipulated the situation, she knew that if she came with someone so powerful and respected within the Bandidos, John would not say anything to cause a scene. I suspected if Mick K knew she was barred and her past history he would never have walked in with her, but the fact still remained she was there flaunting her new relationship with a high ranking member of another club while knowing full well she was barred. So, finally after asking all my questions I still wasn't satisfied the Bandidos were there for trouble. I thought that they must have been drinking at the Pyrmont club house all weekend and decided to visit a few night clubs in order to invite some more girls back to their club house in Pyrmont. I asked John, if they get out of hand do you have enough boys there to handle them? This is where I started to hear the worry in his voice. You see John was only a nom and during all our skirmishes with other clubs in the months before, John was not allowed to get involved, he wasn't even allowed to listen in on our meetings, a nom wasn't privy to all that until he gets his full colours. So,

John didn't know what the situation was with us and the Bandidos, of course he knew that they weren't one of the clubs we were fighting with but he did know that this sort of appearance to his place of work by another club was unacceptable.

As soon as he hesitated in answering me, I knew he wanted my help but wasn't sure if he should ask for it or not. So, I made it easy for him. I told him I will come and talk to them. As soon as I hung up the phone, I called Harry. He was the only other member in the city and the most senior. The phone rang out a few times and I needed to talk with Harry now more than ever. I apologized to Dom and his wife and told them I had something important to do, but I would be back soon. I continued to ring Harry's phone while I got changed; just by habit I wore all black just in case, and in my mind, I was still thinking everything was Ok. I would talk to Sash, let him know it's not a good look having so many of his boys at my nom's place of work. I wasn't even going to mention Angie being there with them, I would deal with her another time.

So, I got changed, said goodbye to Jane and our guests and jumped into the Porsche, drove to the burner around the corner and picked up two hand guns, one black 9mm Berretta and one nickel plated 9mm Smith and Wesson. By this point I still hadn't had any luck in getting a hold of Harry and finally about three blocks away from Harry's house he answers. I told him to get ready and I will be picking him up in a few minutes. As I got to his place, I parked the car right in front and waited for him to come out. When he did, I leaned over from the driver's side to the passenger's side so I could open the door for him. Harry having an ex-military background also came out dressed for action. He knew by the sound of my voice all the missed calls and the precise request to "get dressed I will pick you up in a minute" didn't mean we were going dancing. As soon as he was in the car, I gave him the Smith & Wesson. He did the usual checks to familiarize himself with the weapon and I explained the situation. I made it clear to him I didn't think there would be any problems but he knew as well as I did you don't go into a situation like this unarmed. After filling Harry in, I called Bear to let him know what was happening. He asked the same questions as I did when speaking with John, and at the end, he asked me if I wanted him to drive down. I told him NO straight away, there was no need for it, in my mind I was still hoping it was just a misunderstanding, plus since the thing with the Grave Robbers. Bear wasn't the same, he was using more coke and not making any money; another reason I didn't want his help is because he let me know a few times in paying back money I lent him, so, I wasn't too happy with him, but he was still my brother and those things could be sorted out in the future. After hanging up the phone, I told Harry what I had in mind. The plan was simple, I would get Sash out the front of the Blackmarket to talk to him. As we got to the night club, I parked the car in the side street beside the club. I switched of the engine, took the safety off the gun, half-cocked it, and put it down the small of my back as I got out of the car. Harry did exactly the same. We both knew if there were anyone other than just Sash coming out to talk, they would want to do their normal Bandido greeting where they hug you to say hello but at the same time feeling for weapons, this was something they adopted after Milperra massacre.

We got to the front door and said hello to the bouncers before pulling John to the side to talk to him. I wanted to know if anything had changed since the last time we spoke. Nothing had, so I told him to go inside and tell Sash that me and Harry were here outside and we wanted to talk to him.

As John went back in to pass the message, me and Harry had another chat to the bouncers. They weren't too happy about bikies taking over their workplace and I could fully understand that. I apologized and told them and I would try to sort it out. Just then, John walked back out alone. He told us that Sasha wants to use the cellar to have a chat; and they can have a few lines at the same time. Red flag number 3. Any other time this was not an unreasonable request. Normally, me and Sash would often get into private rooms in many clubs in the City, but only when we were there with one or two other people. This was not a normal situation.

I did not want to go into the Blackmarket, let alone down the stairs to the cellar. But we were there now and we just had to go with it. I had convinced myself that this was just a misunderstanding and as soon as I brought it up with Sash he would apologize and insist we party with them. But all those thoughts would be shattered in 10 steps. Me and Harry followed John into the club and by the 10th step we were at the entrance to the cellar behind the cloak room. There were four Bandidos around that area that I knew. We did the normal Bandidos hug greeting and as

I looked around, I saw a few more Bandidos looking in our direction from the first bar where I would normally sit. And walking away from that group was Sasha, Mick K and Rick DeStoop, Red Flag number 4.

John unlocked the door leading to the cellar and walked in first to make sure there were no staff there. After coming back up he held the door open for us and one of the Bandidos that first greeted us tried to go down first, but Sasha pulled him back by his ponytail and whispered something in his ear. At this point I was seeing red flags everywhere, but there was no turning back. Sash, Mick K and Rick walked down, followed by me and Harry. Once down there, me and Harry put our hands out to shake theirs, first Sash then Mick, who both put their hands out to shake as well. But when I got to Rick, he wouldn't remove his hands from the back of his bum bag even though my hand was already extended.

That was it for me, there was no doubt now this was a very bad situation, and all the cards were stacked against us. My mind was going a hundred miles an hour trying to find a way out of this, so I started talking, at first softly and calmly to see their reaction. I explained that it's not good for the owner and his staff when all you boys come here in numbers like this, and I could see the smug smile on Mick's face. That's when I decided to try and throw them off balance, so me and Harry could get our guns out before they could rush us. It was a very small area, so it wasn't easy, but I started to pace up and down as my voice got louder and my attitude meaner.

I was pacing between Rick and Mick K: two steps forward then I would turn and take two steps back. While

I did this, I started to go off swearing and bringing up every point, like the fact that we have an agreement that you don't come in numbers to a club where other clubs earn their living, and you don't parade that member's ex-girlfriend at a place where she is not welcomed, and on top of that – I turned and pulled out my Berretta and put it to Rick's head as I finished what I was saying – on top of that this cock sucker owes our club money.

They were all stunned but it worked. Me and Harry now had both guns pointed to DeStoop's head. My back was to the caged area where all the booze was kept, and Harry was facing me with his left side facing the stairs. Everyone was frozen. The only sound we could hear at that point was the heavy bass coming from the music above our heads. I spoke again, this time much calmer. I told DeStoop he had three seconds to show me his hands and I started counting. Me and Harry were in a good position now, so if they tried to rush us, we could take them all down easy. But what we didn't expect was another Bandidos hiding on the steps behind the wall before the first landing, where the steps take a 90-degree turn to the left.

So, I am counting: 1, my eyes on everyone; 2, I noticed Sasha looking up to the top of the stairs and at that moment before I could say 3, a number of things happened. The guy on the stair's fires one shot with a small-calibre pistol, hitting Harry in the hand holding the Smith & Wesson. The bullet hits the bone on his index finger between the knuckle and his wrist, bouncing off the bone and hitting the floor. As soon as I hear the first shot, I shoot DeStoop in the head – as does Harry

– killing him instantly. DeStoop drops dead right on top of the projectile that hit Harry in the hand. Then I direct my face to the shooter on the stairs who was still pointing his gun at me, but all I could see of him was part of his head and neck and one hand holding the gun. So, I fired three rapid shots, hitting him three times in the hand and neck but not killing him. He ran off. While I was doing that, Harry fired off two more shots to his right: first one dropping Mick K and the second one hits Sasha in the head as he tries to rush Harry. He only managed to extend his arms and take one step before Harry shot him in the head as well.

So, Harry and I are standing there in the middle of the cellar of the Blackmarket with three bodies lying on the floor. Our ears are ringing from the six loud noises caused by the firing of two high powered 9mm handguns. At the same time, I could feel the beat of the heavy bass coming from the dance floor above our heads. As we stood there for what seemed to be a few seconds, the ringing in the ears started to dissipate as the beat from the music started to get louder. I was running on instinct and adrenaline. The first thing that went through my mind there and then was to pick up all the empty shells. As I bent over to pick up the ones right in front of me, Mick K, who was lying on his back in front of where I was standing, raised himself from the ground making a blood-curdling sound. As he lifted the top half of his body towards me while I was bent down just about to pick up the first shell, this startled the fuck out of me, so I just instantly put one more bullet in his head, dropping him again.

It seems as though the shot Harry fired only skinned Mick K's head, knocking him out, and the bullet I put into him didn't kill him straight away either. He was to live for a further three days after the shooting we would find out later, but at that moment me and Harry just had to find a way out of there. The shock of Mick K getting up while I was trying to pick up the empty shells made me give up on the idea, so, me and Harry looked at each other and agreed it was time to get out.

We knew upstairs was full of Bandidos and it was most likely that they would know by now that there was a shooting downstairs by the shooter that was on the stairs running away with three bullet holes in him, or by the sound of seven loud shots being fired. So, as I went up the stairs followed by Harry; we both kept our guns close to our bodies but partially concealed so not to startle anyone that didn't know what just happened.

As I got to the top of the stairs and opened the cellar door, I realized that no one had noticed anything. Patrons were still dancing and drinking around the cloak room area. I couldn't see any Bandidos so I put the gun down the front of my jeans so I could reach it quickly if needed, and walked out in a casual manner, not attracting any notice. Harry was wearing a coat, so he put the hand that was hit and holding the gun in the right pocket. As we walked out the front doors it seemed as though no one knew what had happened so me and Harry continued to walk around the corner to where I parked the Porsche.

At that point, Harry mentioned to me he was shot in the hand and I remembered asking is it bleed much. His reply was no. As I walked off the footpath to get into the driver's side seat, I see a patrol car coming down the street. My heart starts beating fast again, but I didn't show any panic. I casually opened my door, got in and took my time turning the engine on hoping the cops would just drive passed us. But they didn't. They were cruising very slowly and then as they got closer to us, they stopped right behind us to let me out. I couldn't just sit there so I pulled out, making sure I did everything by the book. As I pulled out, I told Harry to wipe both guns down and be ready.

So, I am at the intersection of the side street with the Blackmarket to my left and my blinker on to turn right. I knew the call would come in at any moment that there was a shooting at the Blackmarket, so I tried not to attract attention while the cops were behind us. I did the normal checks. I knew they were running my number plates and I knew it would come back as leased to a car yard, so that didn't worry me. What worried me was we were getting deeper into traffic and if I got boxed in and they got the call of the shooting we would be fucked. The longer they stayed on my tail the more the chances I could get boxed in. So, I made the decision to lose them.

As soon as I saw an opening, I put my foot down. All eight cylinders fired up and the Porsche took off. Straight away the cops put the lights and sirens on, and the chase was on. My plan was to move far enough away from the cops so we could get rid of the guns. So as soon as Harry cleaned them, I told him to throw them out when I told him. He was ready. It didn't take long for me to get a bit of space between me and the cops, so when I took a corner with the cops about 50 metres behind us, I told Harry to try and throw the first gun into the drain that was coming up before the cops took the corner. When Harry threw the first gun it looked good; the cops didn't see it and it was heading straight for the drain. The second gun went the same way: as soon as the cops were out of sight, Harry tossed it out the passenger-side window straight for a drain. Unfortunately, we would find out later in court that they never made it into the drain.

The chase had been going for a good 10 minutes by now and I could smell the brakes burning up and the oil in the car boiling. The Porsche I was driving was more a luxury car than a racing car, but it did the job for us. I lost the cops, but I was still in the city, so I dumped the car in an alley and as soon as I turned the engine off, I had already picked out an escape route. But Harry just took off before I could tell him. Unfortunately, he ran back out into the main street where the cops were and ended up being taken down by a guy with a pushbike. I on the other hand, took the route I had chosen and ended up on the main road away from where the cops were.

I signalled a taxi, got in and told him to take me to Bondi. While in the cab, I turned my mobile on and called Jane. I told her to pack a bag and go stay at her sisters straight away. Jane never asked questions, just did what I asked. By the time I got there, she was already gone, so I packed another bag, picked up another phone and some money, and I went underground for three months. During this time, I moved around from one safe house to another every two weeks. I stayed in granny flats, house boats and a unit overlooking the Harbour Bridge just in time for the New Year's Eve fireworks.

By February, my exit plan was complete. A false passport was arranged and a booking as a passenger on a container ship was made. The ship was set to go to Japan, so I would be there in time for the 1998 winter Olympics in Nagano, but it just wasn't meant to be. I was on the ship in my cabin, and I was called to see the captain and the immigration officer that was stamping the passports. You see on a container ship back then, you handed over your passport and the proper officials just checked them out and stamped them if everything was in order. But my passport wasn't very good. It started falling apart in his hands.

I was escorted down to where the immigration officer was to explain, but I'd had enough. All that time in hiding had taken it out of me. I didn't care about getting away anymore. I just wanted to get on with it and go to jail. I had felt bad for Harry being there alone this whole time, so I decided I wouldn't run, even though I could have. No cops were called at this stage and I could have walked off the ship anytime I wanted while the immigration officer took me back to the centre to find out who I was. It took them three days because as usual I wouldn't say a word. They didn't even know if I spoke English. But when they got back my fingerprints and found I was wanted for triple murder, it seemed like a giant weight had been lifted off my chest. It was time now for the next chapter in my life.

Jail

On a warm and sunny day on February the 6th, Australian immigration officers handed me over to the NSW police. I was taken to Surry Hills police station for processing.

The lead officer in the murder investigation had read my criminal history so he didn't try the normal procedure with me. Of course, he asked me if I wanted to make a statement, but I told him I didn't want to talk to any of them without my lawyer present. As soon as you say that to them, they aren't allowed to question you anymore.

But the lead investigation officer thought he would try a different approach with me. I had been asking for a smoke ever since I was placed in a cell at Surry Hills, but they wouldn't give me one. I had a full carton in my bag just in case I couldn't buy any on the ship, but they wouldn't give me access to anything from my travel bag. Instead, the lead investigating officer offered me one of his smokes. He opened my cell and took me to a secure area where the patrol cars were parked. He gave me the smoke and started talking to me like he was a star struck fan meeting his rock star. This sort of threw me at first but I quickly worked out his strategy. I wasn't used to cops talking to me like this, but I stood there and listened to him as I smoked his cigarette.

At first, he was telling me about the scene at the Blackmarket when he got there and all the Bandidos that showed up after. He was talking about them like he didn't like them at all. After not getting any reaction from me he changed his tact. He mentioned to me how a certain very well-known underworld figure was very upset about Sasha's shooting and he was rumoured to have put a fair bit of money on my head. I was to run into this underworld figure two years later at Lithgow Correctional Centre; he was in for a double murder. When I mentioned how the cops were trying to use his name to scare me, he completely denied ever putting any money on my head and I accepted that. I didn't believe it at the time, but you can't dismiss anything.

So, the lead investigator went on talking to me like he knew for years and was catching up on old times. As soon as I smoked three of his smokes, I thanked him politely and then told him that he can go fuck himself now. The smug smirk was gone from his face and the personal vendetta against me started that day. I wouldn't have had it any other way.

The next day I was moved to MRRC (Metropolitan Remand and Reception Centre) at the Silverwater Correctional Complex. I was placed in a wing for new receptions. My arrest had been heavily covered by the media so a lot of people now knew who I was. I settled in very quickly and started making inquiries about Harry. I thought he might be at one of the good wings by now and I would try to get there. But I was wrong. It was Harry's first time in jail and I hadn't anticipated that he would fall for the cop's tricks. Apparently, Harry was put on NA (non-association). This was a tactic used to try and make you think that they had your best interest at heart, but in actual fact it was a way of controlling you by removing you from the pack and making you think that if you did this then they would protect you from that, this only worked on people with big charges and first timers, so it didn't surprise me that Harry had fallen for it.

I knew as soon as I spoke to Harry, I could get him out of there, where he was being kept in Darcy 1, straight across from my wing, Darcy 3. When they were doing laundry one day, I snuck out and spoke to him through the doors. He was convinced that he was in the best place to be, but I explained to him it's like being in protection and he can't stay there. As soon as I said that he changed his thinking. He tried putting in application after application, but they wouldn't let him out for his own safety. What I was about to do next went against everything I ever believed in.

I walked up to the officer's counter in Darcy 3 and told them I feared for my life because of my charges, and so I wanted to be put on NA the same as my co-accused Bruce Malcom Harrison (that's Harry's full name). There was nothing they could do. They had to move me to Darcy 1 and put me on NA even though they knew I was just going there to be with my co-accused Harry. So, they moved me to Darcy 1, but instead of giving me the same comforts as Harry they kept me locked in my cell. But that suited me just fine. You don't really know who you're associating with there, so being locked in was like being in segro for me and that sat a bit better in my mind, even though I knew where I really was.

My next step was to convince Harry that we needed to get off NA and get to a normal wing in the general population. It took two weeks, but at the end I put in an application stating that I would not hold corrective services responsible for anything that happened to me if they let me out to the main population. The next day the governor came to see me, and he told me that they were prepared to let me out, but it wouldn't be with Harry. He then asked me if I was still prepared to sign off. I had enough of NA and hiding by this stage, so I told him "yes" and to get me the fuck out of here. I knew if I hadn't convinced Harry enough by now, I would never be able to get him out.

I was taken off NA and placed in Fordwick 9, a wing with two Bandidos members in for drugs. I knew this was a square up for the cop I told to go fuck himself and for the way I manipulated the system to get Harry out of their clutches. So, I picked out someone I thought could get me a shiv (a shiv is a homemade stabbing implement). I was right; he got me two shivs. I put one in each hand, picked out a safe corner of the wing where I couldn't be snuck up on, and I waited for two days. They sat on the top landing looking at me but never made a move. You see there was a long-standing agreement with bike clubs that what happened outside of jail stays outside of jail, but times were changing and the cops and corrective services were employing the old war tactics of divide and conquer like I have never seen before.

Nevertheless, after two days they moved me to a worker's wing and brought Harry over as well. He ended up giving them the same ultimatum, so there we were in a worker's wing, Hamden 17. I still didn't feel right with what I had to do to get Harry out, so I found a job that had access to every wing in the jail and every wing had access to me if they wanted to do something. I was sick of running and hiding so this was my way of making up for that. If someone had an issue with me, then here I was. It wasn't long before the Bandidos tried to spear someone into me. That guy was tabbed on the oval one day and a message was sent to the Bandidos that if they wanted to spear non-members into me or Harry while in jail then all bets where off.

I never had another problem after that. I even worked with one of the Bandidos who was very close to Rick DeStoop. He treated me with respect, and I did the same to him. We both knew on the outside it would be different, but he was respectful enough to honour the agreement all bikies had at the time. Over the next two years until the first trial started, I locked horns with many screws (prison officers), but I was lucky enough to be working for four executive officers in charge of the gym and oval, where I worked as an activity's sweeper. They were all good people and didn't have that mentality that so many other screws had, where they think because they had the power over your freedom then they had the power over your life. I made a lot of them aware this was not the case with me. The officers in the gym didn't need this false sense of power so they didn't have the power trips other screws would so often go on.

My way of dealing with these screws didn't make life easy for me but what the fuck, this is the way I lived my life. If something isn't right, then I will say something. So, two years passed before our first trial, and because of our belief that you never let the law know what goes on between bike clubs, we didn't explain what really happened. We told the court everything but the truth. In our minds it was no one's business but the two clubs involved, even if it meant a life sentence. We were both prepared for that.

Throughout the trial Harry would draw cartoons of the judge and the prosecutor while we were in the dock, and he would pass them to me. Down in the cells we would amuse ourselves by listening to the other people up for murder charges at the Supreme Court try and convince us how innocent they were and how they were set up. I remember playing along one day and telling this guy in the cell opposite us that I was walking to church one Sunday morning after volunteering at the soup kitchen all night, and when I walked by the Blackmarket I saw two big Russians come out of the nightclub holding a pistol each yelling at everyone to get back. I told the guy that as I watched them run off, I noticed they threw away their guns right there on the footpath for anyone to pick up and accidently hurt themselves with, so I picked them up and at that very moment five cop cars came to a screeching stop from all directions. They all got out with their guns drawn and that was how I was implicated in this horrible mistake of mistaken identity. I couldn't believe he ate it up. He was going on about how corrupt the system is and how we were both set up. I didn't know what to say to him after that response.

When we were in the courtroom, I would hear things in evidence that made sense of things that had been playing on my mind since the day of the shooting. Like why did this happen? We weren't at war with the Bandidos at the time so why would they go to the Blackmarket in numbers and disrespect us like that? It seems as though the Bandidos were distributing a very carefully typed letter to all nightclub owners telling them that it was in their best interest if they hired their security from a security firm the Bandidos had set up using members. It looked like they had a very ambitious plan to take control of all the doors of every club in the City, and the only thing in their way was the city chapter of the Rebels motorcycle club.

So, the trial went on. Me and Harry did everything but tell them what really happened, leaving it wide open for the cops to run the trial any way they wanted. At first, they tried to say it was a straight-out execution, but the evidence just didn't fit. Nevertheless, they did succeed at convincing the jury it was murder, so we went down on three charges of murder and one count of attempted murder. The guy that threw the first shot got off scot-free. We were sentenced to 28 years on the bottom, 33 on the top, but three months later my lawyers put in an appeal and I got up, meaning they accepted our points of law. So, a retrial was ordered, automatically giving Harry another go at it.

The second trial went the same way, the only difference being, I was now classified as an extreme high-risk inmate. So, every time I went to court there were four prison officers standing around me in the courtroom and they were all dressed in blue battle fatigues like special forces cops. This did not look good for me in front of a jury. I felt like Hannibal Lecter from *The Silence of the Lambs*, so no surprise I was found guilty again.

I continued to give corrective services a hard time for the next few years, being moved from jail to jail and eventually ending up in a new one they just finished building in Goulburn. They needed high-profile inmates to put in so they could look good for the media.

And that is how I ended up in the Supermax. That's a story to tell another time.

Appendix

SCENES FROM BEFORE THE REBELS

Hellfire

Warning: contains strong sexual content.

One Sunday morning just before I joined the Rebels, I met a friend somewhere to discuss the transfer of a car rental company to my people. I had run into "car rental (CR)" in the Cross on Saturday night. I was looking after DK's runners and going from club to club when I ran into CR. CR was in town with his friends drinking, and we ran into each other at Dancers. I had known CR from previous deals so when we ran into each other he asked me straight away if I could get him and his friends some coke. I told him I could and we started drinking and snorting coke together.

As the night was ending at 5 a.m. I told CR I had to do a few things, but I would like to continue our conversation about his business he wanted me to take off his hands. He had overcommitted himself with other projects and he needed to offload this rental company to someone quick to get some cash – and he knew I always had cash. There were a few more details we had to sort out, so I asked him to meet me at the Blackmarket day club Hellfire. I told him to let one of the doormen know he was meeting me there, and I was off.

I picked up the money off the runners, counted it, paid them and dropped off the money to one of DK's people. It was around 7 a.m. by the time I got to the Blackmarket. I had to meet someone at the airport later that morning, who needed someone with a gun to be with him at all times while he was in Sydney. So, I still had my Berretta tucked down the front of my pants with just the grip popping out but covered by my shirt. I said hello to all the doormen and asked if a friend of mine had come in. They told me he was at the front bar, where I always sat. It was close to the exit and you could see the whole bottom floor from there.

As soon as I walked in, I saw my friend and took up my seat right in the corner of the front bar. As you walk in to the Blackmarket you go through the front doors to a foyer where you pay the girl, then you go through an archway. On the left is another archway that opens up to the front bar, on the right is the cloak desk, and behind that is a door leading down to a cellar. We would often use that cellar for taking drugs. Only people who knew staff could get into that room.

When you pass the cloak desk and head further into the club, you come across the stairs on your right that take you up to the second-floor dance floor and bar. That's where the DJ was as well. Back down the stairs there were two dance floors and an area with two pool tables. The carpet was always soaked in alcohol and very sticky.

But I never went past the entrance area. I could see pretty much everyone coming in and out from where I was sitting because I was in a corner with very little light and the entrance area was well lit. That's also where they had the cigarette machine. I sat with my back up against the concrete pillar that supported the building and allowed for the big glass that covered the corner of the building from the front. This was heavy duty glass and all blocked out so no light got in. To the left of me there was a 12-foot-long bar; to my right was a round table about the size of a car wheel and about elbow high. If I just leaned my ass up against the stool right in that corner, right elbow on the table and left elbow on the bar, it was the perfect position for a security conscious person (or paranoid, you decide) like me.

So, there I was talking to CR, having some water and checking out all the sexy girls coming in from all the other nightclubs all around Sydney. It was getting close to 10 a.m. when I had to meet the "Gambler", the guy I had to look after while he was in Sydney to bet on the horses. He was a Melbourne underworld figure that I would look after every time he was in Sydney. I did this as a favour for a very good friend of mine – let's call him "the Fixer" for now – but back to what happened next. This one incident would distinguish the Blackmarket day club from any other club I have ever been to.

I was sitting there with my left elbow on the bar holding my bottle of water, right arm resting on the table, talking to CR who was facing the bar with both elbows resting on it. He was about one foot away from me because it was getting very busy by this stage of the morning. The rest of the bar area was packed with patrons waiting to get served. As I spoke to CR about meeting up with him Monday morning to look at the books, a girl I had noticed from earlier that morning was dancing with her girlfriends at the dance floor closest to me. I had noticed her because she had been giving me cheeky looks all morning and giggling with her girlfriends. She was also very scantily dressed, which allowed me to get a good look at her body.

I don't know what it was: her cheeky looks and flirting with me from afar all morning or the fact that her skirt was so small ¼ of her bum cheeks were hanging out, but she had me. As I was admiring her body – at the same time talking to CR – she started walking towards me and CR. The bar was packed, and the only gap was between me and CR. This is where it got very hot in the Hellfire day club. The girl came up to me and squeezed in between me and CR to order a drink. I instantly started to get hard because her left thigh was pressing up against my groin. I had to put one leg on the cigarette machine from along the length of the bar and I had to move my other leg so she could get right in there. It was a tight fit, but she squeezed her sexy little bum in there. She was standing on the trot with both elbows on the bar and slightly bent over waiting for the bartender to serve her.

I continued to try and talk to CR but it was no good. All I could think of was her sexy tight bum pressed up against my groin. As I tried to keep the conversation going, she kept on turning her head towards me and giving me that cheeky smile she had been giving me all morning. As she pressed hard against me, she must have felt the gun down the front of my pants. She looked at me in shock but I did not respond to her shocked expression. I just sat up a bit and reached down with my right hand, pulled out the Beretta and repositioned it at the back of my pants down the small of my back because it was getting very crowded in the front. When I brought my hand back, I didn't put it back on the table. I rested it on my right thigh cupping her right bum cheek. This must have driven her wild: the fact that I wasn't all over her like she was used to and the fact that I was carrying. But she took her left hand off the bar, reached down and started to unbutton my jeans. CR was just standing there in shock. He tried to touch her at one point but she was in control and she wouldn't have any of it, moving his hand in an angry manner.

Straight away CR got the message. I continued to gently cup her ass and run my fingers along the contours of her bum cheeks and thighs. As she got all the buttons on my jeans undone, I felt her small warm hand work its way in past my underwear, pushing it to the side by pulling my manhood out through the opening of where you put your right leg through. My cock was so hard I felt it throbbing in her hand. She started to massage it with her left hand as I continued to try and position myself in the best position. I started to also get more adventurous with my right hand by running my fingers in between her bum cheeks until I could feel the wetness and heat coming from her pussy. I also noticed that she wasn't even wearing a G-String.

It was at this point she upped the ante. As soon as my fingers touched her clitoris she started to push and rub her pussy against my hand. Then she did it, she turns towards CR, looking at him straight in the face, and puts my hard, throbbing cock in between her bum cheeks. Still holding on to the shaft of my cock she starts to lubricate her pussy by rubbing the head of my cock in the juices coming out of her pussy and lubricating that whole area between her inner thighs and bum cheeks. All of a sudden, I was inside her. She pushed her ass hard up against my groin and held it there. I could feel her tightening and then releasing her pussy muscles while I was all the way inside her. As I felt her coming, I squeezed both her thighs and pulled her in even further. When she finished trembling and her pussy had stopped spasming she just casually climbed off my still throbbing hard cock, picked up the drink she ordered and walked back to her girlfriends. I quickly put my dick back into my pants and tried to button up. I didn't come but it was the most sexual experience I have ever had. So that's the Blackmarket's day club Hellfire.

I never ended up doing the deal on the car rental company, but I did pick up the Gambler later that morning. I never got that girl's name and I never ran into her again, but I would never forget her.

CPSIA information can be obtained
at www.ICGtesting.com
Printed in the USA
BVHW030215090821
613975BV00005B/135